AUDITING INFORMATION SYSTEMS

Enhancing Performance of the Enterprise

ABRAHAM NYIRONGO

Order this book online at www.trafford.com
or email orders@trafford.com

Most Trafford titles are also available at major online book retailers.

Print information available on the last page.

ISBN: 978-1-4907-5499-4 (sc)
ISBN: 978-1-4907-5498-7 (hc)
ISBN: 978-1-4907-5497-0 (e)

Library of Congress Control Number: 2015903592

Trafford rev. 03/10/2015

Trafford PUBLISHING® **www.trafford.com**
North America & international
toll-free: 1 888 232 4444 (USA & Canada)
fax: 812 355 4082

CONTENTS

To my wife, Clara, and daughters, Susan and Sarah

PREFACE

This book was written out of my information systems audit practice, research, and presentation notes developed for information systems auditing workshops, which were conducted for corporate clients, and information systems audit training sessions at the University of Zambia. Further research and refinement of presentation notes culminated into the publication of this book. Although the book is targeted at new information systems audit practitioners, it is also a good reference book for those already practicing IS auditing.

The main objective of this book is to get IS audit practitioners and students alike to appreciate that IS auditing can be used to enhance performance of our enterprises by providing sound and appropriate assurance services to senior management. The IS auditor's role is not just about compliance and performance testing but also adding value to the enterprise. It is for this reason that the subtheme for this book, 'Enhancing Performance of the Enterprise', was developed. Most of the examples used in this book are focused on emphasising this subtheme.

The other roles of an IS auditor is to be an advisor to management on how information technology is used and adding value to the enterprise through evaluating investment in IT and its returns. Most organisations, if not all, use IT to enhance efficiency and competitiveness, and IS auditors are used to ensure that this requirement is assured.

The terms IS audit and IT audit have been used interchangeably throughout the book to carry the same meaning. Some professional associations prefer to use one term or the other. The word client has been used to mean auditee and engagement letter being applicable to either internal or external clients.

After refreshing your IS audit skills through reading all the chapters in this book, it is recommended that, if you are new to IS auditing, you start your IS audit practice by learning how to conduct an IT general controls audit. This type of audit will give you a broad and good perspective of IS auditing. IT general controls audit is covered in chapter 10.

The IT general controls audit chapter covers key areas which an enterprise requires in order to have an assurance on the performance and status of the IT infrastructure. The ITGC audit can be used to conduct an assessment of the IT environment and make appropriate recommendations to management on the existence and effectiveness of controls which have been implemented. Key areas which may be covered in an IT general controls audit, but not limited to these, include IT governance, IT risk management, information security management, access controls, disaster recovery, environmental controls, change management, and incident management.

Included in this book is a chapter on application controls audit. This is an audit of application systems, such as accounting application systems or enterprise resource planning (ERP) application systems which include integrated modules used to automate business processes. Modern ERP software would include modules like accounting, distribution or warehousing, manufacturing, sales, marketing, customer service, and business intelligence.

Once the IS auditor has assessed the IT general controls audit results as effective and is confident that appropriate controls do exist and are effective, the next task would be to carry out an application controls audit. This type of audit will establish whether the controls in an application system are effective or not. Line managers are normally interested in knowing the results of an applications controls audit because it directly involves business processes which they use every day.

The term 'specialised audits' has been used to refer to other types of audits such as audit of network devices (firewalls or routers), wireless networks, CAATs, databases, operating systems, servers, and specific utilities supporting other systems. Specialised audits are covered in chapter 12.

In this book, there is an emphasis on the use of and reference to IS auditing standards, procedures, and guidelines. In order to carry out an effective audit, an IS auditor is required to make use of best practice standards regularly published by professional associations such as ISACA, the Institute of Internal Auditors (IIA), and many other related professional organisations. IS audit standards, procedures, and guidelines are required in order to ensure that audit work, recommendations, and comments are guided and are within accepted standards or best practice.

Substantive analysis is one type of audit procedure which can be conducted in order to validate certain assertions made by management during an IT general controls or application system audit. Typically, CAATs is one tool which can be used to perform substantive analysis. Often controls may be assessed as effective but may still not be able to detect certain types of weaknesses or errors. Substantive analysis can be used to investigate such errors in collected data. There are other types of substantive analysis which can be conducted to support ITGC and application system controls audits which are beyond the scope of this book.

A good training in IS auditing should be complimented by practice. Without practice the IS auditor may not be able to sharpen his or her IS audit skills. To be a good and effective IS auditor, one requires a variety of skills, such as a good understanding of the business and IT environment, IT governance, performance metrics, information security, IT risk, and project management. In addition, soft skills such as interpersonal skills, interviewing skills, coaching skills, and advisory skills are necessary.

I hope you will find this book interesting and a good introduction to auditing information systems and a useful start-up literature to the young and new IS audit professionals.

Abraham Nyirongo
Christmas Day 2014

CHAPTER 1

Introduction to Auditing Information Systems

Overview

Information system auditing or information technology auditing is the activity of examining or evaluating of information technology systems. IS auditing also involves assessment of compliance with established policies, procedures, standards, controls, regulations, and legislation. You will find a long list of what IS audit is all about especially with the ever-growing use of IT in enterprises. We will take a close look at the various applications of IS audit later in the chapter.

An IS audit can also be considered as a process of gathering and examining evidence of an organization's information systems practices and operations. The evidence obtained from such a review would help determine if the IT systems are secure, compliant, provide protection to data, and ensure effective and efficient IT service delivery.

It is important to realise that information systems are the lifeline of enterprises that are highly dependent on IT systems. Typical examples are banks, stock exchanges, or airlines. These enterprises operate real-time systems and cannot do without the use of IT systems for more than a few seconds; otherwise, this would entail worldwide disruption of services. The level of automation in such enterprises is usually end to end meaning that most of their business processes are automated.

Because of huge investments and dependence on IT systems, it is important that management keeps an eye on how IT systems are used and operated. This calls for a systematic way of ensuring that IT policies and procedures are implemented and monitored. Senior management requires assurance from time to time that IT systems are being used efficiently and are adding value to the enterprise. This assurance can be provided through the use of information system auditors who are called to regularly examine information systems and associated policies, procedures, practices, and advise management on the status of the systems. IS auditors not only are invited to examine information systems but can be used to conduct various other types of advisory services, which we will review later in the chapter.

Enterprises often implement IS auditing either by setting up an internal IS audit function or use an external IS audit firm. Later in the book, we will assess the benefits and disadvantages of using either audit organisation.

IT risk is a key requirement when an enterprise is implementing an IS audit framework. Before an IS audit framework is implemented, it is important that an IT risk policy is in place. The IS auditor should have a good understanding of the nature of IT risks and how they are being mitigated before developing an IS audit program. We will analyse IT risk in more detail in chapter 6.

History of IS Auditing

The advent of microcomputer systems brought about increased dependence on the use of IT systems by private and public organisations in the mid 1960s and early 1970s. The increased dependence on IT systems also brought in the need to ensure that systems were reliable, secure, and processed data with high accuracy. The use of computer auditors was one way which was considered to enhance assurance and saw the birth of a new profession, which today has hundreds of thousands of practicing IS auditors around the world. The development of IS auditing as a profession was also largely influenced by the growth of the use of computerised accounting systems and the need to have effective IT controls which would provide assurance to management on financial record-keeping in an automated environment.

Today we are seeing the development of large integrated information systems used by multinational corporations such as Microsoft, Samsung, Citibank, and many other similar corporations. These corporations, due to the volumes of transactions, are able to generate large volumes of electronic data. Big data has become a subject of discussion in many enterprises as this has created new opportunities to analyse data and extract various types of information which enterprises can use to enhance performance of their businesses and have a competitive advantage in the marketplace.

The growth of IS auditing has also been influenced by the increasing use of the Internet to conduct business by many enterprises. Most business transactions today are conducted using the Internet, and global enterprises have taken advantage of the Internet to grow and offer their services to a global market.

The original focus of IS auditing was very technical and was more concerned with the technical features of systems than it is today where our focus is more risk-based and centred on the need to enhance business performance.

Accounting scandals in the USA and Europe also reinforced the importance of using IS auditing. IS auditing is used by many enterprises that are dependent on information technology, and it is also highly influenced by various forms of corporate regulations and legislation by jurisdictions around the world.

ISACA is one of the professional organisations which are promoting the practice and development of the information systems auditing profession. The association has been in operation since 1969 when it was incorporated. The Institute of Internal Auditors is one other professional association responsible for promotion of IS auditing. The two organisations collaborate on development of many professional standards and guidelines. There are many other professional and private (for profit) organisations who are involved in the development and practice of IS auditing.

IS auditing is a new profession compared to other professions such as law, accounting, and medicine. The future of IS auditing is dependent on the use of IT systems by enterprises. Every sign indicate that IS auditing is here to stay and will grow with the growth of usage of IT systems in organisations. No one can dispute the fact that IT systems have changed the way enterprises conduct business and that these systems should be regulated to ensure protection of client information and also compliance with many complex legislations being enacted by governments around the world.

Many IS auditors did not join the IS auditing profession straight from college or university but could have joined the profession after many years as external or internal auditors. Many could also have come from other professions such as information technology, accounting, or other business backgrounds. The IS audit profession has grown compared to what it was forty or more years ago. Many large- and medium-sized enterprises today do have IS audit functions or internal auditors performing IS audit responsibilities.

The future of IS auditing can also be assessed from the job market demand for IS auditing professionals. There are many enterprises looking for IS auditors with various skills, from general IS auditors to specialist IS auditors, in areas such as IT security, IT governance, databases, application systems, and networks.

The benefits of implementing IS auditing whether in a small, medium, or large organisation are many, and it is no longer an option but a must to ensure that systems are secure and used to support business goals.

An enterprise which is using and dependent on IT systems to produce business information or automate business processes require the use of IS audit services. Management of any enterprise, small or large, requires to place reliance on IT systems, and this can be effectively done through the use of an IS auditor. A small- or medium-sized enterprise does not necessarily require to employ full-time IS auditors but can consider using the services of external IS auditors or an independent or part-time IS audit consultant who can equally do a good job.

Many medium to large enterprises have full-time IS audit functions supervised by a director or manager. They may also have full-time IS auditors specializing in various areas of IS auditing. Many IS audit functions also provide support services to other functions, such as financial auditing, information security, or risk management.

The IS audit profession is growing, and one can say it is reaching maturity level in that it is now driven and moderated by various standards and guidelines. Governments in the USA, Europe, and other parts of the world have developed legislation which requires the use of IS auditing in order to ensure use of effective IT controls in public organisations and private enterprises enlisted on the stock exchange.

Types of Information Systems Audits

There are various types or reasons for conducting information systems audits as indicated earlier. In the next two pages, we will review the common types of IS audits (see figure 1.1) which are used in most enterprises. You will discover later that IS audit can be used to support various types of advisory work.

#	Types of Audits	Category
1	IT General Controls Audit	General
2	Application Controls Audit	Information Systems
3	IT Governance Audit	IT Governance
4	IT Investment Audit	IT Governance
5	IT Risk Audit	IT Risk Management
6	Information Security Audit	Information Security
7	System Development Audit	Information Systems
8	Business Continuity Audit	Information Security
9	IT Performance Audit	IT Governance
10	Compliance Audit	IT Governance
11	Specialised Audits	Information Systems

Figure 1.1 Types of Audits

IT General Controls Audit

This is a general review of global controls in an IT environment. There are a number of areas which are covered using an IT general controls audit, such as access controls, compliance with internal policies and IT procedures, environmental controls, and disaster recovery. IT general controls audits may be performed to support or in conjunction with financial statement audits, internal audits, or other forms of attestation.

When an IT general controls audit is used to support financial audits, IS auditors would be requested to perform an ITGC audit so that they give assurance to financial auditors on the existence and effectiveness of IT controls. Once IT controls are determined to be effective, financial auditors may consider going ahead with the audit and review financial data.

IT general controls audits can also be performed to give a general assurance to management on the effectiveness of IT controls without any additional specialised audits. Management might want to just have a general picture of existing IT controls and their effectiveness. The IT general controls audit will be reviewed in more detail in chapter 10.

Application Systems Controls Audit

This is an examination of IT controls in an application system such as an accounting package or ERP system. An application systems controls audit involves examining specific application systems used to automate business processes. An enterprise might have one or more application systems which are used to operate the business. In many cases, enterprises today are opting for integrated systems, such as ERP systems, compared to using non-integrated systems which require multiple data input.

There are a number of areas which are covered during an application systems controls audit, such as input controls, processing controls, output controls, access controls, and disaster recovery procedures.

Application systems controls audits can either be conducted in conjunction with an IT general controls audit or a specialised audit. An application systems controls audit is specific to a particular business process or processes and requires specialised skills. It is normally recommended that an IS auditor auditing a financial system should also have training in that particular application system in addition to having general IS auditing skills. This topic will be considered in more detail in chapter 11.

IT Governance Audit

IT governance is about ensuring that IT is aligned and supports business goals, good management of IT risk, appropriate investment in IT infrastructure, and use of IT to achieve a competitive advantage or creation of business opportunities. Enterprises that have implemented IT governance have witnessed a number of new opportunities. You may have also noticed that small or medium enterprises would not like to remain behind in the effective use of IT which results from implementing IT governance.

When auditing an IT governance framework, IS auditors focus on areas such as involvement of the board of directors in IT governance, investment in IT, how regular IT is discussed at board and management levels. The IS auditor would also look at how IT strategy is aligned to business strategy. One other important area is to assess how IT governance is translated into IT management and operational strategies at management and operational levels. This topic will be reviewed in more detail in chapter 5.

IT Investment Audit

This is an evaluation of an enterprise's investment in IT infrastructure in order to determine returns from the use the IT systems. Returns can be determined by savings resulting from automation of business processes or the use of new or more efficient and effective IT systems. Savings can also be determined from use of fewer employees because most processes are now being performed by computers. Returns can also be determined from use of less paper in the office. Instead of sending paper invoices, the new system can make use of email to send invoices electronically or copies of invoices can be accessed on the company web portal.

There are a number of other factors that can be used to determine returns on IT investments. Sometimes it is difficult and not so obvious as automation might increase operating costs, such as the requirement of highly skilled employees who might command a higher salary. One might also think of increased network connection fees to link the head office, branch offices, and business partners.

IT Risk Audit

IT risk audit involves an evaluation of how IT risk has been implemented and is managed in the enterprise. Effective management of IT risk is a key requirement in any IT environment. An IS auditor would review an IT risk profile of an enterprise by looking at IT risk policies, procedures, and the IT risk register. The IS auditor would be looking for evidence that risks have been properly identified and mitigated. The IS auditor would also be looking for evidence of risk awareness across all levels in the enterprise. This topic will be reviewed in more detail in chapter 6.

Information Security Audit

In our interconnected world, security risks are ever increasing, and enterprises are vulnerable to various threats especially those hosting sensitive client data. Enterprises are required to put in place effective security measures which will ensure that the IT infrastructure is properly secured.

Information security auditing involves reviewing areas such as network security, database and application security, protection from viruses, website security, and intrusion detection. The IS auditor will also be looking at how secure the IT systems are from both internal and external threats. An information security audit also covers protection of a number of information types, such as information in soft copy, hard copy, voice, and video.

Information security is an important aspect of the enterprise, and management normally calls for security audits to be held more frequently than other audits. In some enterprises, security audits are real-time and security auditing is a continuous activity. This topic will be analysed in more detail in chapter 7.

System Deployment Audit

IS auditors are often required to get involved when systems are being developed and implemented. This is to ensure that the systems being deployed have all the required security and IT controls included as specified in the system specification. It is common to find developers or integrators missing out one or more features on a new system even when such features are in the specifications. In order to avoid such costly mistakes, it is important that auditors are involved when new systems are being deployed in the enterprise. IS auditors should also be involved when major changes are being made to business systems.

The IS auditor, in order to maintain independence, may be required not to get involved in the actual design of the system but to only review implementation and ensure that the development team is complying with user and system requirements. This topic will be considered in more detail in chapter 8.

Business Continuity Audit

Business continuity and disaster recovery audit is the review of the enterprise's preparedness in the event of a disaster or incident impacting on the operations of the enterprise. Business continuity and disaster recovery can also be reviewed when carrying out an information security audit. The audit on business continuity focuses on policies, plans, implementation, and monitoring of business continuity and disaster recovery plans. In this book, we will make a comprehensive review of disaster recovery in chapter 9.

IT Performance Audit

IT performance audits require the use of appropriate IT metrics as tools for assessing performance of the IT function and infrastructure in the enterprise. Regular audits of how the IT function and infrastructure is performing enables management to determine how IT is contributing to the success of the enterprise and how IT goals are being achieved. IT service delivery is one of the key activities which can be used to assess performance of the IT function and supporting systems. IT performance audits also can be used to complement assessment of investment in IT infrastructure.

IS auditors are required to perform IT performance audits in order to determine areas of improvement in IT service delivery and also look for evidence on how IT services are impacting the overall performance of the enterprise. A compliance review can also be performed within an IT performance audit in order to assess compliance with established performance metrics.

Compliance Audit

One of the common audits which are regularly performed by IS auditors are compliance audits. These audits normally evaluate the organisation's compliance with IT policies, procedures, regulations, and legislation. IT policies and procedures are a creation of the enterprises whilst regulations and legislation would be enacted by governments or other authorities. Compliance audits add value to the enterprise as they ensure good standing in the market and community they operate in. Compliance audits also assist in mitigating risks which the enterprise might be facing.

Specialised Audits

Specialised audits are audits which require specialised skills and normally go beyond the requirements or scope of the IT general controls audit. Examples of specialised audits would include auditing firewalls, databases, cloud hosting infrastructure, real-time security systems, proprietary application systems, and use of audit software to perform substantive analysis such as CAATs. We have used the term 'specialised audit' in order to distinguish this type of audit from other audits which do not require specialised skills, such as the IT general controls audit. This topic will be reviewed in more detail in chapter 12.

IS Auditing Skills

After considering the various types of IS audits which are at the disposal of the IS auditor, it is important to also look at the skills required to be a good and effective IS auditor.

In order to be an effective IS auditor, one requires a combination of a number of skills. In many cases, specialist skills are required to perform specialist audits, such as auditing a demilitarised zone (DMZ) for a global online retailer such as Amazon.com.

Most employers looking for SAP IS auditors would insist that job applicants, apart from being CISA-certified, should also be certified in SAP, which is a fair requirement and applies to most application systems. IS auditors need to receive specialist training in the system they are auditing in addition to general IS auditing skills.

Listed below are some of the skills required for an IS auditor to be able to perform his job effectively.

a) Project management – An IS auditor should have good project management skills to be able to plan and execute his IS audit projects effectively and successfully.

b) IS audit process – The IS audit process is about how to conduct an IS audit from planning to reporting. This is a general skill required for the IS auditor to be able to conduct an audit effectively. A detailed review of the IS audit process is covered in chapter 2.

c) IS audit standards – An IS auditor can be effective if his audit work is based on accepted best practice, such as making use of standards and guidelines. Organisations such as ISACA and IIA have published various standards and guidelines for use by IS auditors in executing their work. An IS auditor requires a good understanding of IS audit standards and guidelines. A detailed review of IT audit standards is covered in chapter 3.

d) IT risk – One of the components of the enterprise risk management framework is IT risk. The IS auditor is required to understand the IT risk profile of the client and how it has been implemented. A detailed review of IT risk is covered in chapter 6.

e) IT governance – The IS auditor is expected to understand the IT governance framework and related standards and guidelines such as ISO 38500, ITIL, and COBIT. The understanding of IT governance is important for an IS auditor as it enables the auditor to be able to conduct an IT governance audit and assess how IT governance influences IT management and operations.

f) Information security – Understanding of information security is key for an IS auditor as most type of audits have a requirement to review security implementation and operations. Most auditing training courses, including the most sought after CISA certification, has a security module.

g) Flair for technology – In order to be a successful IS auditor, one requires to have a good flair for technology. An IS auditor cannot conduct a successful audit without having a good understanding of technology. Technology is ever changing, and new technologies are introduced on the market every time. An IS auditor cannot afford to remain behind and not understand new technologies on the market.

h) Specialised training – In addition to general IS auditing skills, an auditor may chose to specialise in various specialist areas, such as information security, IT risk, IT governance, networking, firewalls, databases, and application systems.

The business education market has noticed the growing need for IS auditing skills such that they have now introduced various degree courses at bachelor's and master's level. This is in direct competition with professional bodies which have been offering certification courses for many years, such as ISACA and the Institute of Internal Auditors (IIA).

All auditors need to have an understanding of IS auditing whether as a financial internal or external auditor because of the wide use of IT systems in automating business processes. We are seeing a number of accountants taking up IS auditing as a profession or a combination of the two.

After reading this chapter, you might be thinking of taking up a course and write an exam in IS auditing, if you are not already CISA or CIA certified. You are on the right path. By the time you reach the last chapter of the book, you will have a firm foundation of IS auditing. There are various types of certifications which you may consider. Some are specific to IS auditing whilst others are more specialised in other areas such as information security, IT governance, and IT risks.

One way of enhancing your standing as a professional IS auditor is to study for one of the following certifications. You will be required to sit for an examination and also have professional experience in order to be officially certified. Listed in figure 1.2 below are the some of the major IS auditing professional certifications.

#	Certification	Examining Body
1	Certified Information System Auditor (CISA)	ISACA
2	Certified Internal Auditor (CIA)	IIA

Figure 1.2 IS Auditing Certifications

There are also other IS audit–related certifications you may consider in the areas of IT governance, security, and risk management certifications listed in figure 1.3

#	Certification	Examining Body
1	Certified Information Systems Security Professional (CISSP)	$(ISC)^2$

2	Certified Information Security Manager (CISM)	ISACA
3	Certified in Risk and Information Systems Control (CRISC)	ISACA
4	Certified in the Governance of Enterprise IT (CEGIT)	ISACA
5	Certified ISO 27001 Lead Auditor	ISO
6	COBIT	ISACA

Figure 1.3 IT Assurance Certifications

CHAPTER 2

Information Systems Audit Process

Overview

A skill the IS auditor needs to learn quickly and be able to perform perfectly well is how to use an IS audit process. This chapter looks at the various stages of performing an IS audit. Adding value to the enterprise or enhancing performance of the enterprise requires being able to conduct a good IS audit in the first place.

The IS audit process includes a number of activities which ensure that an effective audit is carried out. Described in this chapter is a generic IS audit process, but it does meet the required objectives as described in the IS audit standards and guidelines published by ISACA and the Institute of Internal Auditors (IIA). Enterprises in some cases prefer to design their own audit process focusing on their internal requirements. Further details on the IS audit standards will be covered in chapter 3.

The IS audit process involves a number of stages (see figure 2.1), which we shall review in detail in this chapter. The IS audit process includes the following stages:

a) audit planning
b) understanding the IT environment
c) performing the audit
d) testing and evaluation
e) findings and reporting
f) follow-up.

Figure 2.1 IS Audit Process

The benefit of using an IS audit process when performing an audit is that you ensure that the audit has a structured approach which everyone can follow including clients. The process enables a clear understanding of the objectives and tests included in the audit. The IS audit process also helps the IS auditor to avoid errors or missing out important information during the auditing process.

Audit Planning

The purpose of the planning stage is to ensure that the IS auditor has a plan which will assist the IS audit team conduct the audit in an orderly and efficient fashion. Not so much as in military precision but in an orderly manner taking into consideration all the relevant activities required to perform an IS audit.

You will remember what we covered in chapter 1 regarding what type of skills an IS auditor requires to perform an audit. Project management was one of the skills we mentioned. Planning is a project management activity and is a key skill required to manage an audit engagement. Where an audit team consists of many members (let's say ten or more auditors), it is good practice to use a project management software to manage the audit project. There are many types of project management software at the disposal of the IS auditor with the popular one being Microsoft Project. There are also free open-source project management software which can be downloaded from the Internet. Project management software has many useful features, such as being able to list project activities, project dependences, and apply timelines to each activity.

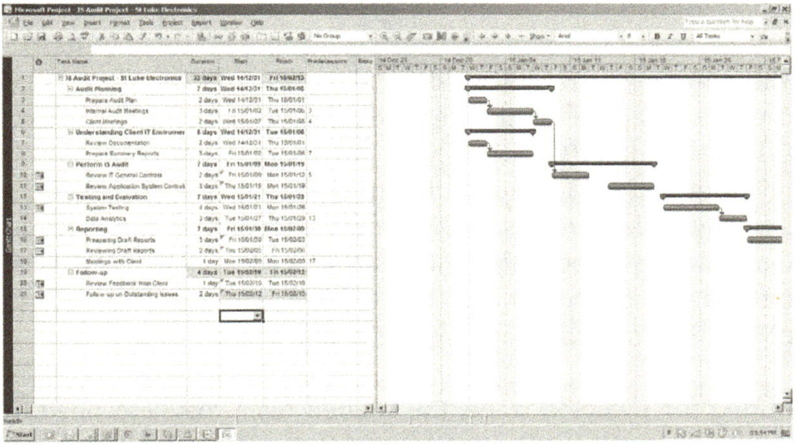

Figure 2.2 Project Activity Schedule

Some major activities during the audit planning stage include holding internal planning meetings as the IS audit team and also holding kick-off meetings with the client. It is important that during the planning stage, the audit team holds internal planning meetings to discuss how the audit would be executed. The IS audit team leader may chair the meeting and explain the audit objectives and logistics of the audit. During this meeting, the audit team will also agree on the audit schedule and required resources. The planning meeting is usually attended by all members of the audit team. The meetings can also be used to explain the objectives of the audit to the rest of the audit team and discuss the requirements of the engagement letter and expected deliverables.

It is also useful to hold kick-off meetings with the client so that the engagement letter can be clearly explained to the IS audit team. At the kick-off meeting, the client or user department will attempt to explain their IT environment and any challenges they have had. The audit team will seek clarifications at this meeting regarding the audit objectives or any other issues relevant to the audit. The meetings can also be used to discuss reporting timelines and report formats if any.

The meetings can be used to discuss expectations of the client and agree to the required deliverables and content. Disagreements often occur with the client because of having different understandings or interpretation of the engagement letter and deliverables. It is recommended that the IS audit team should effectively utilise the kick-off meetings to seek clarifications on the engagement letter or terms of reference to ensure that misunderstandings are minimised.

During the planning stage, the IS audit team may also need to determine if there is a requirement to involve specialists, such as data analysts, security experts, computer forensic specialists, and database specialists. Specialists are required to assist the IS auditors where the IS audit team does not have particular competencies. We will look at the involvement of specialists in more detail in chapter 12. ISACA has published a standard on the involvement of other auditors and specialists. IS auditors should take into consideration the requirements of this standard, which we will review in more detail in chapter 3.

Other than planning documents which are required to be collected during the planning stage, the IS auditor is also required to plan for resources which would be used during the audit such as number of IS auditors, other experts, logistical support, and audit tools such as audit work paper software, data analysis software, and testing tools.

At the end of the planning stage, the IS auditor would have collected a number of documents which should be reviewed in order to have a good understanding of the client's IT environment. This information and knowledge will enable the IS auditor to perform an effective and value-adding audit.

Developing Audit Objectives

Understanding and knowing how to develop audit objectives is a necessary skill for an IS auditor as this can help in conducting audits effectively and according to the requirements of the client. A misunderstanding of the audit objectives may lead to performing an audit which does not meet the expectations of the client and run the risk of the final audit report being rejected.

Audit objectives specify what the IS auditor is required to do or achieve on a particular audit engagement. Audit objectives may be developed for an entire system or for a specific part of an IT system. Management might provide one or more objectives which are linked to expected deliverables. Including specific deliverables to the engagement letter or audit request memo helps in developing a clear understanding of the expectations and avoids misunderstanding with management. Problems IS auditors usually encounter in practice is making recommendations, which sometimes are different from management expectations, due to not having a clear understanding of audit objectives.

IS auditors sometimes find themselves in a position of advising the client on how to develop audit objectives. The following may serve as general guidelines when developing audit objectives:

a) The IS auditor should be provided with sufficient information on the client's business and IT environment.
b) The IS auditor should have access to the enterprise IT strategy, organisational structure, IT policies and procedures.
c) The area or function to be audited should be clearly described and in sufficient detail, i.e. network infrastructure could be the selected area to be audited.
d) Audit objectives should be detailed enough to guide the audit team.
e) Deliverables should be clearly stated and linked to audit objectives.
f) Reporting timelines and report formats should be provided.
g) Consideration should be given to developing sub-objectives relating to performance, compliance, security, monitoring, maintenance, and management. Management may opt to focus on one or two metrics such as compliance and performance.

The engagement letter or audit request memo should include the following information for it to communicate appropriate information to the IS auditor:

a) general overview expressing the issues at hand and areas of focus
b) list of audit objectives (and sub-objectives where necessary) in action format
c) agreed reporting format if the enterprise does not have a reporting template
d) expected deliverables
e) dates for reporting.

The benefits of having clearly defined audit objectives include having a clear understanding and agreement between the IS auditor and management, avoiding disagreements during reporting, and avoiding delays in implementing recommendations.

Audit Methodology

IS auditors can consider using questionnaires as a method of collecting data during an audit and presented to the client in an interview format. This method enables the IS auditor to be organised and be able to collect all the necessary information without missing out any key pieces of information. The questionnaires also enable the IS auditor to follow an orderly pattern and look organised to the client.

It is advisable to develop a questionnaire following the same sequence as the audit objectives. Each audit objective should have a number of questions depending on the depth of audit required. Where necessary, include to each question some guidelines on what evidence should be collected to support the response from the client. In order to avoid having too much information on the questionnaire, any additional information and comments can be moved to the end of the questionnaire.

A questionnaire should enable the IS auditor to collect sufficient information so that he is able to make appropriate observations and recommendations to management. For example, if the IS auditor is auditing a database system, he might be required to review the following areas:

a) database schema
b) access controls
c) use of triggers
d) data privacy
e) disaster recovery

f) change controls
g) database audit trail
h) integration with other systems.

Each area may require five to ten questions if all necessary information is to be collected. Depending on the experience of the IS auditor in auditing databases, additional questions might be fielded during the audit.

Remember that an audit is not just about presenting questions to the client. The IS auditor should ensure that the responses are supported by appropriate evidence, and the evidence may need to be tested as a further way of validating the responses. We will look at evidence testing and validation later in the chapter. It has been observed in a number of audits engagements, both financial and IS audits, where auditors use the questionnaire as a checklist without further probing the auditee with specific questions on the performance of a particular system. General questions will not enable collection of critical information required by an IS auditor to make informed recommendations.

It is important to remember that all questions should lead the IS auditor to collecting sufficient information to make appropriate observations and recommendations on each audit objective stated in the engagement letter. It is the responsibility of the IS auditor to develop a good questionnaire which will be used to collect information on a particular audit. In already established IS audit departments, standard questionnaires would have been developed by other auditors or consultants and can be used in repeat audits.

Whilst questionnaires may be good tools which can be used to collect data, it is recommended that IS auditors consider making use of other tools, such as observing systems at work, analysing data captured from live systems, or comparing performance of similar systems.

Understanding the IT Environment

As part of planning activities, it is important that the auditor has a good understanding of the enterprise to be audited. The IS auditor should understand the nature of the client's business and operations before setting out to develop the audit program. The IS audit team may not perform a good audit if they are not familiar with the client's business and IT environment. This requirement applies to both internal and external IS auditors. It is easier for internal IS auditors to have access to enterprise information than external auditors. Extra effort need to be applied for external auditors to collect all the required information. Often you will find a situation where the client may not be willing to provide all requested information for various reasons.

Key information an IS auditor would be looking for is the business strategy of the organisation. The strategy would outline what the business intends to do or is doing to achieve its overall goals. The client would provide this information through a business strategy document approved by the board. It is likely that the CEO or any member of senior management would have a copy of the strategy document. In the business strategy document, the IS auditor will find the IT strategy of the enterprise. In some enterprises, the IT strategy could be a separate document (separated for easy access). The IT strategy outlines how the enterprise is using IT to deliver on promise or provide IT services.

Additional information an IS auditor would need during this stage are supporting IT policies and procedures. The IS auditor should have a clear understanding of the IT polices in place so that he is aware of how IT operates and is used in the enterprise. The IS auditor will be expected to use IT policies to assess IT compliance and operations.

A key document required during the audit is the business process document. This could be a separate document, or the processes could be described as part of procedures in a procedures document. The document will outline all the business processes which are used to carry out business operations. Business processes are normally expressed as procedures (manual or automated). In a highly automated environment, most of these processes would be configured as processes in an application system. The IS auditor may be required to review the business processes so that he has a good understanding of business operations.

The IS auditor may also be required to look at the financial regulations obtained in the enterprise especially if the audit will involve reviewing the accounting application system. IT operational procedures covering the enterprise resource planning (ERP) or any other application system may also be required for review. IT operations procedures are included in the IT operations manual. This document can be found with the IT director or manager.

Before the IS auditor commences the audit assignment, one important document required is the audit charter. The document outlines the organisations' audit statement or policy. All audits to be conducted in the enterprise should be guided by the audit charter. This document is normally found with the audit director or any member of senior management. The audit charter will have a section on IS audit. In some enterprises, you might find an IS audit charter as a separate document but linked to the main audit charter. In addition to the IS audit charter, the IS auditor may be given an engagement letter which will outline audit objectives and expectations which are specific to the area or system to be audited.

The IT department is a good area to start the IS audit from as it gives the IS auditor a first-hand impression of the level of IT controls in the enterprise. Documents required when reviewing the IT organisation in the enterprise include the organisation structure, job descriptions, authority levels, user rights, segregation of duties, and section roles within the IT department.

The IS auditor may also collect additional information on available controls in the systems in use. Usually the IS auditor will find documented IT controls which are either in hard copy, soft copy, or embedded in the systems. The IS auditor should be on the lookout for undocumented controls, which sometimes do exist where old systems are in use or new systems which were not properly implemented. In such a case, the IS auditor may decide to conduct a preliminary interview with IT management in order to establish the existence of undocumented IT controls.

There are many other documents not mentioned here which the IS auditor may be required to collect and review during the planning and IT environment review stages. The guide would be the engagement letter provided by the client.

The planning and understanding the client's IT environment stages help in ensuring that the IS auditor has a clear picture of what is required during an audit engagement. These are key stages which should not be skipped or ignored. There is always a tendency by new IS audit practitioners to go straight into performing the audit, which often results into disastrous outcomes.

Performing the Audit

This is the stage when the actual audit is performed by the IS auditor using various tools. This comes after the planning, IT and the business environment assessment stages have been successfully concluded and a go-ahead has been given to start the audit. The IS auditor would start by making interview appointments with the relevant officers, such as the IT director, IT manager, line managers, data and systems owners. It is advisable or good practice to commence the audit with senior management such as the CEO, IT director, IT manager, or line managers so that issues relating to IT governance and other major IT issues affecting the enterprise are discussed first. Later the IS auditor can proceed with interviews with operations staff, such as IT system managers, systems administrators, network administrators, and application administrators.

Armed with well-developed questionnaires and audit tools, the work of an IS auditor should be a lot easier and a happy journey throughout all the offices and departments. As the IS auditor makes appointments to interview various managers and specialists, he should remember that his work is that of an advisor and a value-adding IS auditor. The IS auditor should not be seen as a police officer or somebody who has come to find faults. Immediately the IS auditor is perceived to be taking the policing role, It is likely that the officers would resent his presence and might receive limited cooperation from the auditees. An assurance from the IS auditor that he is there to add value at the commencement of the audit will help provide the required assurance and enable them to open up and fully cooperate. It is important that the auditees receive assurance from the IS auditor that he is there to help them enhance performance of the enterprise. In many instances, the auditees will even volunteer more information than required if they have confidence in the IS auditor.

During the audit, the IS auditor will be required to collect evidence supporting responses from the client. Where the client is not able to provide evidence immediately, it is good practice to write down in the questionnaire (just below the questions) the type of evidence you will be collecting later after the interview. This will help the IS auditor to later compile a list of documents to collect. The IS auditor should not rely on others to be reminded of this responsibility. Everyone is busy, and it is unlikely that they will send a reminder notice.

In addition to collecting responses and evidence in document form, the IS auditor will be required to make data extracts from live or backup system. It's good practice for the IS auditor to extract data from a non-production system where it is not practical to extract data from a live system. Data can be extracted from backup servers or from the recovery site. Sometimes the IS auditor might be required to observe live real-time systems. In this case, the IS auditor and the client will have to make sure that the connection to the live system is well tested and will not disturb or corrupt the live system. The IS auditor should also request for appropriate authorisation from senior management before extracting data from the live system.

In cases where authorisation is not given by senior management, the IS auditor may have to rely on historical data from backup servers. It is also recommended that only suitable and approved software is used to interrogate or connect to live servers.

There are various data interrogation tools on the market which can be used to support different types of audits. The IS auditor can find on the market special software tools which are used to extract data from network devices such as firewalls, routers, switches, and intrusion detection systems. Software houses have also developed specialized software which can be used to extract and interrogate data from different databases such as MS SQL, IBM DB2, Oracle, and MySQL.

An IS auditor will also come across dedicated tools which are used to extract data from applications systems such as financial or ERP systems. There are free open-source and commercial versions available on the market. Data can also be extracted from audit trails or other systems which record user activities on application servers or network operating systems. Common data extract and analysis tools on the market include ACL, IDEA, and Excel. There are also many other non-commercial software which can be used.

The purpose of audit software interrogation tools is to extract data so that it can be analysed and investigated for input and processing errors, data integrity, fraud, and data corruption among many other reasons. Often IT controls may not be able to identify these errors, and there is a need to use such software as validation tools.

Data stored on servers and data silos hold a lot of information and can tell a lot of hidden stories if properly interrogated. It is also the role of the IS auditor to drill down into these silos and advise management on how business activities are carried out in the enterprise and whether there are significant issues which need management's attention.

Most applications and operating systems have inbuilt tools which flag off errors and other unauthorised activities in addition to the use of audit trail tools. It is almost unforgiveable in any modern enterprise today to implement an ERP system which does not have an audit trail unless other measures have been put in place to gather similar data or perform the same function.

Testing and Evaluation

Once the audit has been completed through structured interviews, use of questionnaires, observations, walk-throughs, and collection of necessary evidence to support management attestation, the next activity would be to test the information and evidence collected. Before the testing is performed, it is important that the IS auditor reviews the documents and evidence checklist to ensure that all the necessary information has been collected.

Testing involves validating the responses and evidence the IS auditor collected during the audit. Compliance testing is the easiest as it involves confirming whether the enterprise is compliant with various IT policies, procedures, regulations, and laws. The process involves comparing what is expected and what is obtained on the ground. Where the enterprise is not compliant, the auditor will take up the issue for discussion with management and possible inclusion in the final report.

Other tests may involve assessing whether performance standards are being achieved by the enterprise. Performance standards may relate to service levels, maintenance, and monitoring.

Testing may include system testing to ensure that configurations have been implemented according to approved standards. An example would be checking that a firewall configuration was implemented according to accepted standard. Testing a firewall may include conducting a penetration test. An auditor may also check that a database system was configured with the required security hardening standard. Testing systems is more demanding and might take up most of the auditor's time.

The IS auditor may also test whether IT systems are being monitored by IT management. This would involve asking the IT department to show records indicating which systems were monitored, what their findings were, and what was reported to management. Normally IT departments would have in place monitoring procedures for various systems which indicate what is being monitored and how often the monitoring is being done and what type of data is being collected during monitoring.

During testing the IS auditor will also be looking for evidence that backups are being carried out and signed off by a senior supervisor. It is normally not safe and sufficient to assume that backups are being carried out through word of mouth. The backup operator should record in a logbook or other system that backups are being taken and reviewed by a senior supervisor or manager. The auditor will also be looking for evidence that the backups are tested for restoration. It is pointless to make backups which cannot be restored.

Access controls also need to be tested in order to ensure that all users have appropriate access rights on the systems they are using. User accounts are created and removed every time, and access rights also change due to changing job requirements. Testing that access controls are implemented correctly is one of the regular tasks of an IS auditor.

The IS auditor would take particular interest in auditing change management. Change controls also need to be regularly tested in order to ensure that all changes are properly implemented and documented. It is common to find that changes are not documented or tested before being implemented.

Findings and Reporting

The next activity for the IS auditor after performing the audit and evaluation of findings is to write up a report to management. The report should address the audit objectives outlined in the engagement letter or audit request memo in case of internal IS auditors.

It is always advisable that the audit report is prepared in good time and sent to the client on the agreed dates. Where this is not possible, communication should be sent in good time, indicating that the report will not be ready on the agreed date and reasons given on why the report will be delayed. It is always good to avoid the report being rejected on the basis that it is late by communicating with the client if there are challenges regarding the preparation of the report.

The IS auditor and the client would have agreed on distribution of the report prior to commencing the audit and most likely during the kick-off meeting. It is important to adhere to the agreed distribution so that the report is not sent to unauthorised persons.

This is especially more important if the report is going to the board as the report might contain sensitive issues.

One of the controversial issues in most audit meetings is concerning the report format. In some enterprises, preference is given to detailed reports while others accept brief reports. Normally higher level managers prefer less-detailed reports than lower operational or technical levels. It is also important to take note of the report formats used in the enterprise. It is good practice to follow the client's report format if it does not pose any significant challenges.

The IS auditor should also be aware of organisational politics at various levels. Reports sometimes are rejected because the audit director and IT director have personal differences or because one of the senior officers did not agree to the terms of reference or audit objectives.

It is accepted practice to report on what has not been achieved or complied with. In some enterprises, management might demand for more information, which includes the entire picture of the IT environment. This is a requirement which should also be agreed before commencement of the audit, whether the report should focus on excerpts only or provide the whole picture.

The IS auditor should take note of the importance of using balanced language in the report. If the recipients are not very technical, it is good practice to use non-technical language unless it is not possible to avoid use of technical words. Where the recipients are technical, it is recommended to use technical language so that the client is able to provide appropriate technical responses to the IS auditors. Where the auditor would like to support the observations and recommendations made with detailed technical data (such as diagrams, specifications, and maps), it is advisable to move such detailed information to the appendix.

Indicated below is the possible report structure which could be used to prepare an audit report. There are different types of report structures you could use, and some may be specific to particular enterprises. In some enterprises, especially those with an international presence, they prefer to have uniform reporting tools across all their offices.

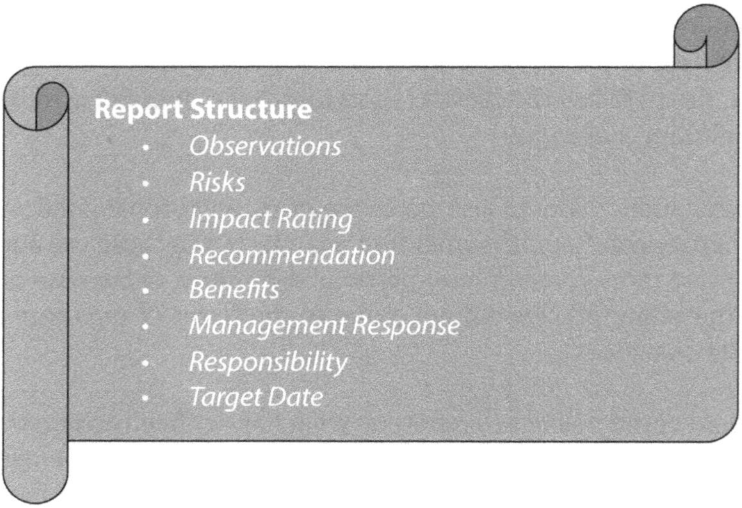

Figure 2.3 Report Structure

Observations – The IS auditor should use this column to indicate what he has observed relating to a particular activity. The statement should be made as an observation because the auditor is basing the statement on available information at the time of the audit. The observation should be detailed enough and, where necessary, supported by evidence collected during the audit. If the supporting evidence documentation is large, the IS auditor might consider including the evidence in the appendix.

Risk – Allows the IS auditor to indicate the risk to the enterprise of the observation. The IS auditor may include one or more risks identified.

Impact Rating – The impact rating can be high, moderate, or low. Higher impact rating may indicate that immediate action should be taken and with an appropriate level of mitigation. It is advisable to include the impact rating so that the client is aware of the level of impact regarding a particular observation.

Recommendations – The IS auditor should make clear recommendations in order to enable the client to implement the recommendations. Often clients will ask how the implementation should be carried out if they are not clear with the IS auditor's recommendations.

Benefits – Benefits indicate what rewards would be derived from implementing the recommendations. It is important to add benefits in the report as it motivates the client to appreciate the importance of your recommendations.

Management Response – This is the response management gives on the IS auditor's observations. Management might agree or disagree with the observations and recommendations made by the IS auditor.

Responsibility – This indicates who is responsible for implementing the recommendations made by the auditors. This could be the system owner, the IT director, finance director, or functional head.

Target Dates – It is always important to agree with the client on the dates for resolution of the issues raised in the report. This will allow the auditor to follow up on or after the indicated dates.

At the end of the audit, the IS auditor would have collected a number of documents and also generated new documents. Listed below in figure 2.4 are the various documents and pieces of information the IS auditor would have collected during your audit.

a) Audit charter or IT audit charter
b) Engagement letter or audit request memo
c) Business and IT strategy documents
d) Business process documents
e) IT policies, processes, procedures, and standards
f) Audit questionnaires with collected data
g) Evidence in form of data extracts
h) Evidence in form of compliance documents
i) Data on tests carried out
j) Completed audit report to management

Figure 2.4 List of Audit Documentation

Follow-Up

An IS auditor is required to follow up on issues raised in the audit report either immediately after the audit or on agreed dates with the client. A follow-up can also be made just before commencement of a new or next audit. The IS auditor should review implementation of the recommendations made in the previous report. If previous recommendations were not implemented, the auditor can include in his new audit report which issues were still outstanding and the reasons why the recommendations were not implemented.

The IS auditor might consider reporting on how previous recommendations were resolved in the new report. In some enterprises, this section is moved to the appendix as it is for information only so that the new report focuses on new issues being raised.

In some cases, the IS auditor might find that the same issues keep on coming up in every audit. It is advisable that these issues are escalated to senior management or the board for special consideration. It is only right that the enterprise takes a position of either accepting the risk or resolving the issues raised in previous reports.

An IS auditor is at times found in a position where the client is disputing observations made regarding a particular issue. In this case, the auditor might refer the issue to the client's board for resolution. This is on the assumption that the audit team has extensively reviewed the issue and strongly believe that they have a strong point and supporting evidence.

All issues which have been resolved need not be reported and should be dropped unless management would like to keep them on record, indicating reasons how the issues were resolved.

CHAPTER 3

Use of Information Systems Audit Standards

Overview

In our review of how standards are applied or used in an IS audit, we shall refer to the IS audit process pyramid diagram depicted below (figure 3.1). Under each activity, we will indicate which standards and guidelines are used. It is recommended that you read chapter 2 before reading this chapter.

Before we look at the various standards and guidelines, let us first define what the two terms mean. We shall use definitions made by ISACA.

A standard is a mandatory requirement, code of practice, or specification approved by a recognized external standards organization, such as International Organization for Standardization (ISO) (ISACA Glossary).

ISACA says that standards are mandatory in all cases. The term 'shall' indicates 'must'. Any deviations from the standard must be addressed prior to completion of the IS audit (ITAF, 2nd edn, ISACA, page 6).

A guideline is a description of a particular way of accomplishing something that is less prescriptive than a procedure (ISACA Glossary).

ISACA says guidelines are not mandatory but adhering to them is strongly recommended. Although they do allow IS audit and assurance professionals a degree of application freedom. Professionals must be able to defend and justify any significant deviation from the guidelines or the omission of relevant sections of the guidance in the conduct of IS audit and assurance engagements. This is particularly true if the engagement is more at the IS audit level. Not all guidelines will be applicable in all situations, but they should always be considered (ITAF, 2nd edn, ISACA, page 6).

All the standards we will be referring to in this chapter can be found on the ISACA website IT audit and assurance standards page. It is advisable that you download the ITAF second edition for reference as you read through this chapter. Standards use 1000 (for general standards), 1200 (for performance standards), and 1400 (for reporting standards) series code. Guidelines use 2000 (for general guidelines), 2200 (for performance standards), and 2400 (for reporting standards) series codes. It is important to remember these codes so that you are able to distinguish between standards and guidelines.

With this full understanding and distinction between standards and guidelines, let us look at which standards and guidelines apply to each stage of the IS audit process as shown in figure 3.1.

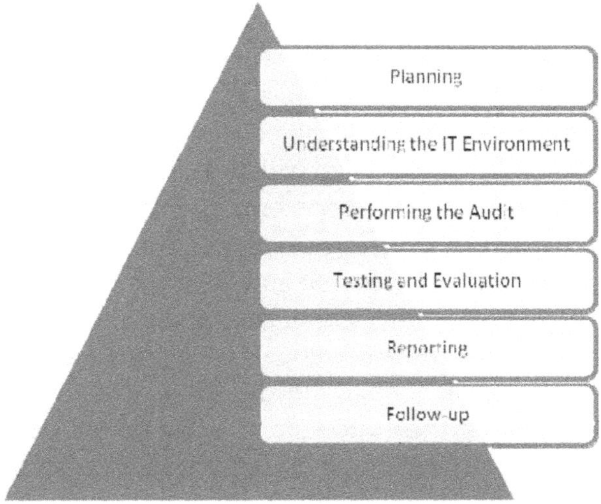

Figure 3.1 IS Audit Process

Planning

Planning is an important activity when performing an IS audit, and it enables the IS auditor to prepare for the audit adequately. In chapter 2, we covered various tasks required to be undertaken in order to develop an effective audit plan. In this chapter, we shall try to identify various standards and guidelines which are used during the planning stage.

It is assumed that the general standards (1000 series) are applicable to the entire IS audit program, and where necessary, we shall refer to the standards in the various sections reviewed in this chapter.

Engagement Planning (1201.1 and 1201.2)

During the planning stage, there are two standards relating to planning an engagement which an IS auditor must adhere to. These are mandatory standards.

The 1201.1 information system audit standard requires IS auditors to develop a plan for every IS audit engagement they have been requested to perform. The plan should include audit objectives, the scope of the audit, schedule, and deliverables. It is important that the audit objectives are clear and normally would be discussed and agreed with the client during the kick-off meeting. Determining the scope of the audit is one of the main activities during the planning stage. The scope can be used to determine the limits of the audit and what the IS auditors can do on the audit. Without the scope, auditors would find it difficult to estimate the schedule of activities. Deliverables are the end product of an audit normally in the form of reports. Auditors should ensure that they understand what the deliverables are and when they are required to be submitted. Late submission of deliverables and submission of reports which do not meet the client's expectation usually send a wrong signal to the client.

IS auditors are expected to also understand and incorporate into their audit program compliance with applicable laws and professional auditing standards. Governments from time to time come up with regulations and legislation to ensure that the citizens or public resources are protected. In some cases, laws may be updated to reflect current requirements. Enterprises also come up with internal policies and procedures which auditors might be required to follow. Professional associations such as ISACA or IIA, on the other hand, also develop auditing standards which auditors are required to follow. IS auditors are required to be current with applicable laws and professional standards. One of the requirements to be certified as an IS auditor by ISACA is acceptance to observe standards, association by-laws, and to be professional in approach to work.

During the planning stage, it is recommended that the IS auditor uses a risk-based approach where necessary. The auditor would be guided by the enterprise risk profile or any risk assessments which were performed in the recent past. Time allowing, the IS auditor can perform an independent risk assessment in order to validate some information in the risk reports. A review of the various risk reports and a discussion with the risk manager or any member of staff with enterprise risk management responsibilities would suffice.

It is always advisable that IS auditors address engagement-specific issues when conducting an audit. Digressing from the provided audit objectives would not only cause the audit to take longer but be in conflict with expectations of the client. The IS auditor also runs the risk of having the deliverables being rejected because they have included issues outside the scope of the engagement.

IS auditors during the planning stage also should be clear as to what documentation and reporting is required. This information would be included in the engagement letter and should also be verified with the client before the audit starts. Where this information is not available, it is the responsibility of the IS auditor to ensure that this information is made available by the client.

The 1201.2 information system audit standard requires that the audit team should develop and document an IS audit or assurance engagement project plan. The IS audit plan can easily be developed using project management software such as Microsoft Projects. The project software would enable the IS auditor to indicate the tasks, schedule, and resources to be used on the engagement.

IS auditors should take particular interest regarding the nature of the engagement as this would determine how to approach the work and how to address the audit objectives. Audits which involve compliance with the enterprise IT policies and procedures may not require use of special software to perform the audit. Although at the higher end, compliance work may require the IS auditor to hold interviews with the board or senior management which could require good skills and approach as he deals with senior executives. So the nature of the engagement might demand for certain types of audit skills and procedures to conduct the audit engagement effectively.

Risk Assessment in Planning (1202.1 to 1202.3)

The 1202.1 information systems audit standard requires that an appropriate risk assessment approach and supporting methodology be used to develop the IS audit plan and determine priorities for the effective allocation of IS audit resources. Risk assessment is one of the tools required to assess risk in the enterprise and can also be used to identify critical assets. Priority and allocation of resources can be determined based on the risk level, which can be high, medium, or low. Criticality of IT assets and impact are other factors which can be used to assign priority of allocating audit resources. Risk assessment should be included from the planning stage and cover all other stages of the IS audit process.

The 1202.2 information systems audit standard expects IS auditors to be careful when assessing risk on individual areas or IT asset as the risk has to be relevant to the area or asset. It is advisable that the auditors first gain an overall understanding of risk in the enterprise before they perform risk assessment on individual IT assets. Some risks may be relevant to particular assets and might disappear when a number of assets are considered as a single unit.

During the planning stage, IS auditors will be required to ensure that (1202.3 information systems audit standard) consideration is given to subject matter risk, audit risk, and related exposure to the enterprise. Subject matter risk is risk directly related to the asset or area being audited. Audit risk is the possibility that information or reports may have material errors which the auditor may not have detected.

In practice, subject matter risks can be identified by carrying out a risk assessment on the subject area or IT asset. This could be based on the design and effectiveness of IT controls or compliance with security standards and regulations. Audit risk often does occur where inexperienced auditors or non-specialist auditors are used to perform audits which require particular skills. A good example would be allowing a generalist IS auditor to perform an audit requiring SAP skills. The audit team should ensure that, during planning, auditors with appropriate skills are used to avoid audit risk, although it is not a disputed fact that audit risk exposure can happen even where experienced auditors are involved.

Performance and Supervision (1203.1 to 1203.3)

The use of a carefully developed (1203.1 information systems audit standard) audit program will ensure that the audit is not exposed to unnecessary risks. Use of project management software will help to ensure that the audit is kept within the approved schedule.

Where an audit program is out of schedule, it is important that a review is made and necessary corrections are made and approved by both the IS audit team and the client.

The 1203.2 information systems audit standard requires auditors to ensure that all junior or trainee IS auditors are supervised in an appropriate manner so that professional IS audit standards are maintained. The authors of the standard had in mind the need to achieve audit objectives as agreed with the client. Providing sufficient guidance and training to IS audit staff is key to maintaining the requirements of this standard. During planning, the audit team shall ensure that appropriate supervisory controls are built in the audit program.

The 1203.3 information systems audit standard extends the earlier standard by requiring that the IS audit team ensure that staff with appropriate knowledge and skills are used on the engagement. The standard does allow the use of audit staff that might not have the required skills to work on the engagement under supervision. This is common in most audit functions due to unavailability of skilled staff and also the deterring factor of high salaries demanded by experienced auditors.

Materiality (1204.1)

The 1204.1 information systems audit standard requires that IS auditors consider, at the planning stage of the engagement, potential weaknesses or absences of IT controls that could result in a significant deficiency or a material weakness. The use of IT general controls audit is one method which can be used to assess absence or weaknesses in IT controls. ITGC will give a high-level overview of the level of IT controls in the enterprise or particular subject area being audited.

The IS audit team might decide that before they perform any other audit, they should consider performing an ITGC audit. This activity may be incorporated in the audit plan and performed at the early stage of the audit. If the ITGC audit results into an assessment which indicates significant deficiency or a material weakness, the audit team may decide to halt the audit and advise the client.

Using the Work of Other Experts (1206.1 to 1206.2)

The IS audit team should assess and decide during the planning stage (1206.1 information systems audit standard) whether the team requires the use of other experts in performing the engagement. It is important that the audit team makes a careful consideration as using other experts will increase the value of the audit as other experts will be able to provide high-level skills which are not available on the team. Other experts would include, for example, data analysts, computer forensic specialists, database specialists, SAP application system experts, network specialists, and firewall security professionals.

The 1206.2 information systems audit standard requires that the IS audit team should ensure that the other experts to be used on the engagement have the skills to perform the support audit. The other experts will be bringing to the audit team skills which the other team members do not have. It would defeat the sound objective and approach of the IS audit team if inexperienced and unqualified experts were used on the engagement.

In a case where the IS audit team has an engagement of auditing databases in the enterprise which store data used by the core application system, the IS audit team might require special database skills to perform the audit. The engagement letter might require the IS audit team to perform a more detailed audit, such as testing Oracle database alerts and triggers, data transfers between databases, and account mapping. In this case, the other experts are required to have good competencies in Oracle database design and administration in addition to general

IS auditing qualifications and experience. The IS audit team will determine what type of assistance they need on the audit engagement from the other experts.

The required skills from the other experts might include professional qualifications or certifications in the area of assignment. It is recommended that the other experts also have specific competencies and experience in the area of assignment. Competencies and experience refer to having previous experience in similar work and environment.

If the other experts are required to review CISCO firewalls, it would be required that the experts should have appropriate competencies in CISCO firewalls. Depending on the type of work to be carried out, the experts should also have appropriate experience such as two or three years experience working in the area under review plus general information systems auditing experience. The IS audit team should also ensure that the other experts have appropriate resources to conduct the audit, such as software tools, audit templates, and are using approved audit standards and guidelines.

In order to carry out an effective IS audit, the audit team should also ensure that the other experts are independent of the enterprise or department being audited and the audit team. This will allow them to make independent and impartial recommendations to the audit team. Independence will also give the audit team and the client the required confidence on the opinion provided by the experts.

A key requirement when engaging other experts is the need to ensure quality control and compliance processes are observed prior to the engagement taking place. These include the experts signing confidentiality agreements, which would compel them not to disclose client's confidential information. The other requirement would be for the other experts to sign a conflict of interest statement, which would confirm that they have no specific interest in the enterprise or department being audited. The statement should be prepared in a professional manner so that it is clear to both the client and any other parties who might request access to the statement.

Understanding the Client's Business and IT Environment

Understanding the client's business and IT environment is an important requirement at the planning stage. The two have been deliberately separated so that we can have a detailed review of the subject areas. It has been observed that many IS auditors pay little attention to details presented at the planning stage either because they feel that they already know most of the information or because they are performing a second or third audit for the same enterprise. A good understanding of the client's environment will enable the IS auditor to clearly understand the audit objectives as prescribed by the client and also perform the audit more effectively.

ISACA has developed standards and guidelines which can be used when reviewing the client's environment such as 1201 and 1202 standards. These standards require that during planning, the IS auditors take into consideration the requirement to have a good understanding of the enterprise. It is important that the IS audit team develops a good understanding of the client's business strategies, operations, and risks. This will help the IS audit team have a good understanding of the enterprise and focus the audit in the areas of high risk.

A good starting point would be to review the client's business environment. The IS audit team might consider reviewing the entire business environment or a specific area. Where the engagement is focused on auditing an application system, which does not concern the whole enterprise, the audit team might choose to review the business environment only related to the focus area. Where an IS audit team is reviewing an end to end ERP system, reviewing the entire business environment might be the preferred option. Information to be collected during the review of the business environment might include previous audit reports by internal and external auditors. Other internal reports would also be a good source of information. The IS audit team might also collect business strategy documents, business processes documentation, organisational policies, financial reports, risk management reports, performance reports, and any other business reports the audit team might find useful.

After obtaining a good understanding of the general business environment, the audit team will be in a position to review the IT environment. Remember that the purpose of the IT function is to support the enterprise and not the other way round. Depending on the audit objectives, the focus might be on a particular area or the entire IT environment. The selection of a focus area will depend on the type of system being audited. If the system affects the entire enterprise, the audit might cover the entire business environment. Where the system is specific to a particular department or area, the audit might focus on specific areas.

The IS audit team is required to review and understand the IT environment by first reviewing the internal IT organisation. The review would include the IT organisation structure, segregation of duties, and IT operations. The IS audit team might also be required to review documentation such as IT strategy document, IT policy document, IT standards, and IT procedures used in the enterprise. These documents will enable the IS audit team to develop a good understanding of the IT environment.

The IS audit team might also consider reviewing partnerships and alliances with outside enterprises who are suppliers of various IT services to the enterprise. Such suppliers might have service-level agreements with the enterprise which may also entail having access to the enterprise IT infrastructure.

In order to ensure provision of efficient customer services, most enterprises provide online services and support to its customers. Online procurement of goods and services with minimal human contact is common in most enterprises and it is a preferred method as it is more efficient and reduces on labour costs. The IS auditor should take an interest in how such services are delivered and how related IT risks are managed.

Other external interfaces which need to be considered during this stage include regulators, vendors, and consultants. All these external contacts may require access to the enterprise IT infrastructure. It is imperative that issues of IT controls, security, and privacy are considered before the audit commences. The IS audit team would be required to review agreements with the suppliers, consultants, and vendors. The IS audit team should consider reviewing the existence and content of service-level agreements, if any, between the enterprise and its suppliers. Lastly, the IS audit team should also consider reviewing how the client's business processes are impacted and modified by these various agreements or relationships.

The 1204.1 information systems audit standard requires auditors to consider potential weaknesses or lack of controls at the planning stage so that they can determine any substantial materiality. This information should be considered at the planning stage and would help indicate what to include in the plan. Where materiality is considered to be high, the IS audit team might decide to extend the test of controls by conducting substantive testing procedures, such as using CAATs.

A high level risk assessment during the planning stage may be performed in order to provide assurance that all areas with high materiality have been included and would be reviewed during the audit. The risk assessment should include a review of the enterprise's IT environment. The IS audit team should also take into consideration inherent risk the organisation is facing.

The IS audit team might consider looking at the risk profile of the enterprise in order to determine the risk levels. The team should also review other risk documents such as risk governance, risk policy, and procedures.

At the end of this stage, the IS audit team would have reviewed and obtained a good understanding of the organisation's environment and also collected sufficient information to assist in the refining of the audit plan.

Performing the Audit

The next stage after collecting all the necessary information about the enterprise is to perform the audit. The IS auditor would also have collected all the necessary tools required on the audit. Communication with the client and all members of the IS audit team is important so that everyone is aware of what is expected of them. The key document is the audit plan which could be in the form of a project management plan developed using Microsoft Projects or other similar software.

The audit plan would include timelines and resources to be used during the audit. The plan would normally be broken down into tasks, and each task would have resources allocated to it and the duration for completion of the activities.

It is important to secure appointments with the various officers you intend to meet during the audit in good time. It is quite disappointing for one to go out for an audit and not be able to find the right people. Not only can this situation disrupt an IS auditor's audit plan but also requires him to schedule another trip to meet the auditee.

It is recommended that the IS audit team provides sufficient information to the client prior to the meeting. For example, it would be good to advise the client which areas the IS auditor will be reviewing on each particular day. The full program of the IS auditor's activities should also be communicated to the client in advance. If the IS auditor has planned to review the network environment on the first day, communication with the client should be made in good time so the client is able to have all the necessary information ready and also facilitate access to various networking devices and IT rooms. In some cases, network servers might be the responsibility of a different person, and such information needs to be relied to the appropriate person in good time in order for the second person to prepare for the audit.

The client might also require to be informed how the IS auditor would like to collect the evidence or data. If the IS auditor would like to collect data from a firewall monitoring tool for example, he will need to indicate whether the data should be provided in printed copies or soft copies. Some enterprises have internal policies which do not allow distribution of soft copies to third parties. These issues need to be cleared early with the client so that it does not become a stumbling block during the audit.

It is usually good practice to prepare questionnaires in advance before the IS auditor commences the audit. This gives the IS auditor an assurance that all areas of the audit would be covered. Well-prepared questionnaires also allow the IS auditor to field further questions to the client which can be recorded on the questionnaire itself. The questionnaire should cover all issues relating to the audit objectives. There is usually a tendency during interviews to get carried away and ask questions which are outside the scope of the audit. The IS auditor is required to develop a number of questions for each audit objective which will enable collection of appropriate evidence to support responses from the client.

In addition to questionnaires, the IS auditor might collect information through walk-throughs and observation of various activities taking place or confirming existence of various devices which might have been installed, such as routers, firewalls, and network switches.

The IS auditor might require using software tools to interrogate the client's systems so that evidence can be collected. The audit team and the client need to agree what software tools the auditors can use and how connection to the client systems would be made. In some enterprise, it is preferred to use offline systems (backup servers) which contain the same data as the live system.

The 1203.4 ISACA information systems audit standard requires that IS auditors collect sufficient and relevant information in order to achieve agreed audit objectives. Collecting evidence is quite a demanding exercise, and sufficient time should be allocated to this activity.

The 1203.5 information systems audit standard requires the IS auditor to document the entire audit process, and this information will be used to support findings and recommendations which will be made at the end of the audit. It is also important to document all activities during the audit as this information is required for future reference and audit records. In some countries, audit records are required by law to be kept for seven or ten years before it is destroyed. Clients may also want detailed information to support the IS auditors conclusions and recommendations. Detailed information can be accessed from the records kept during the entire audit.

Testing and Evaluation

After performing the audit and collecting necessary evidence, the IS auditor has the task of testing and evaluating the evidence collected. The testing and evaluation stage can also be performed during the actual auditing stage. In this book, the two stages have been separated so that we can review the two areas in more detail. At the end of the chapter, you will see the benefits of separating the two stages of performing the audit and carrying out testing and evaluation of collected evidence.

At this stage, the IS auditor will test or examine the collected evidence in order to find out whether the design of the controls was properly done and that the controls are effective. The IS auditor will be using data or evidence collected when performing the audit to test the controls. Substantive tests can also be performed on data collected from the system in addition to testing the design of IT controls. Other tests can also be performed depending on the client's requirements.

The 1203.6 information systems audit standard requires auditors to identify and conclude on findings. This is done after testing the controls to determine their effectiveness. Auditors can also evaluate IT performance or operations against IT policies, processes, and procedures in order to identify and conclude on findings.

If, for example, the finding is that the risk is high of being hacked after performing a network infrastructure audit due to some vulnerabilities, the IS auditor might consider carrying out further testing (substantive testing) such as a penetration test in order to test if the enterprise is secure and all ports not in use on the firewalls and routers are closed.

Another example where further testing is required is when the risk is considered high on an ERP system for possible inaccurate postings by accounting staff. The IS auditor may consider carrying out data analytics using CAATs tools, such as ACL, IDEA, or Excel, to confirm the accuracy of data being captured on the ERP system. A data input walk-through would be another way of carrying out further tests.

IS auditors can also perform compliance testing against set policies, procedures, and standards. For example, information security policies can be tested using ISO 27001 security standard.

IT performance testing is one other common test. The IS auditors would collect evidence in the form of actual performance results from a system and compare it with planned performance which was set by the management team. The difference in results will enable auditors to identify possible findings and make recommendations. Of course sometimes it could be 100 per cent good performance. Performance metrics can also be used to assess IT performance.

When conducting testing of evidence (1204.3 information systems audit standards), it is important to consider the overall effect of minor control weaknesses and whether the absences of controls qualify into a significant material weakness. The overall effect should be based on a particular audit area. For example, the overall effect of minor control weaknesses on a network infrastructure. The result could be high or low material findings.

The 1205.1 information systems audit standard requires that IS auditors obtain sufficient and relevant evidence to enable them to make appropriate conclusions on which to base their findings and recommendations. If evidence is limited, it may be difficult for the IS auditor to make convincing conclusions and recommendations to management. Where management has a different opinion, it might be challenging for the auditor to justify the recommendations without sufficient evidence.

The audit team needs to ensure (1205.2 information systems audit standards) that evidence collected is sufficient to support conclusions and achieve engagement objectives. This means that conclusions should be based on evidence collected and not otherwise. It is the role of the IS audit team to ensure a sound evaluation of the evidence collected and using appropriate evaluation criteria.

Audit findings can be accepted if the assertion made by the auditors is supported by evidence obtained. It is important that audit objectives are clearly understood and agreed at the beginning of the audit if the client and IS auditor are to achieve and accept expected results of the audit. Normally disagreements arise if the client and the auditor have different interpretation of the audit objectives.

Findings and Reporting

After the audit has been performed and testing of evidence has been completed, the next stage is to produce a report to the client. The 1401.1 information systems audit standard requires the IS auditor to communicate the results of the audit upon completion of the engagement. The standard also specifies the recommended content of the audit report (ISACA 2013) which includes the following:

a) identification of the enterprise or organisation being audited

b) the intended recipients and any restrictions on content and circulation should be clearly communicated

c) the scope, engagement objectives, period of coverage, and the nature, timing, and extent of the work performed

d) the findings, conclusions, and recommendations should be clearly written

e) any qualifications or limitations in the scope that the IS audit and assurance professional has with respect to the engagement

f) signature, date, and distribution according to the terms of the audit charter or engagement letter.

The 1204 information systems audit standard goes further by stating that the findings in the report are supposed to be supported by sufficient and relevant evidence. This has been discussed in detail in the earlier sections of this chapter.

The structure of the report may vary from one enterprise to the other, but the basic information contained in the reports should be the same. It is important that the language in the report should not be very technical if the recipients or part of the recipient group are not technical people. Where all recipients are technical, it is fine to use high-level technical language as long as it does not hide the main objectives of the report. The idea of a report is to communicate findings, recommendations, conclusions, and not the technical language.

For the report to be an effective tool of communication, it should carry clearly written observations or findings in line with the audit objectives, ending with recommendations and conclusions.

Distribution of the report is also important. Only authorised recipients should have access to the report. Many times unauthorised people have received IS audit reports causing problems for the IS auditors and sometimes the client.

It is always important to include an executive summary in the report for use by the board or senior management, who might not have the time to read the entire report. Sometimes management would want to make a quick decision and might find the summary suitable for such purposes.

A detailed review of the report structure has been included in chapter 2. It is advisable to review this chapter so that you can have a clear understanding of the audit reporting structure.

Follow-Up

Many IS audit writers have combined this stage with the reporting stage, the one we considered just before this stage. As earlier indicated, we will consider this stage as a separate stage, as it is useful in practice to handle this stage separately.

The 1402.1 information systems audit standard requires that auditors make follow-ups on whether management has taken action regarding reported audit findings and recommendations.

Management might not implement the recommendations immediately after the report is produced and opt to implement on agreed dates. In this case, the IS audit team might develop a planned follow-up action schedule which the team can use to make follow-ups. It is always important to recommend to management response criteria. High-risk areas would require immediate action whilst low-risk areas may require action at an agreed date.

The IS audit team should agree with the client on the findings and recommendations in the report and develop an action plan on how to implement the recommendations. This should be done immediately after the report is released or at the first audit report review meeting with the client.

In case of audits conducted by external auditors, it is good practice to make use of internal IS auditors to make follow-ups which they can include in their work schedule. The external auditors can follow up at a later date with the internal auditors or during their next audit.

Where there are disagreements on particular findings and recommendations, management and the IS audit team can opt to escalate the issue to senior management or the board for resolution.

The follow-up activity is important as it enables the IS auditors to find out if their recommendations are being implemented and that there is improvement in the operations and performance of the enterprise. It should be a source of concern to the IS auditor if recommendations are not being implemented.

CHAPTER 4

Information Technology Review

Overview

A flair for technology is one important attribute for being a good and successful IS auditor. New technologies are always being developed, and enterprises are also rapidly adopting new technologies in order to enhance performance, competitiveness, and profitability.

In this chapter, we will review some of the key technologies used in an enterprise. To be a successful IS auditor, a good knowledge of information technology is required, and always keeping up to date with new developments in the technology sector is recommended. It would be difficult for an IS auditor to provide appropriate recommendations and conclusions if his understanding of the IT environment is limited. Most of the reviews the IS auditor would perform concern compliance and performance, which require evaluation of various technologies in use and those available on the market.

IS auditors, in some cases, will be required to have advanced technical understanding of systems they will be auditing. A basic understanding of technologies will not be sufficient to perform highly technical audits. In such cases, IS auditors are required to undergo specialised training in systems such as SQL database system, IBM DB2 database systems, CISCO networking, or Linux operating systems.

The IS auditor should regularly read professional journals, books, and other technology literature in order to keep abreast with technology. There is so much literature on the Internet, which is freely accessible, and many professional organisations including universities have dedicated vast amounts of resources to develop peer-reviewed materials which can be useful to IS auditors.

It is a good approach to conduct background research on technologies used in an enterprise before commencing an IS audit, as it allows the IS auditor to have good technical background information on the systems in use.

IS auditors should be mindful that the state of technologies used in enterprises may be at different stages. Some enterprises may be interested in mature technologies because they are tested, reliable, and used by many other enterprises. Other enterprises may prefer to use emerging technologies because they are cheaper and, in many cases, offer new opportunities. The IS auditor will also find some enterprises using a hybrid IT environment where matured and emerging technologies are in use.

The focus as we review these technologies will be from an IS audit perspective. We will first review the general description and application of the technologies used in an enterprise and then later look at the possible audit objectives for each type of technology, including the expected outcomes for auditing such systems. IS auditors should understand the technologies from the audit perspective as this is what they will be encountering in their everyday audit work.

This chapter has been structured in such a way that we will first review technologies which are used to access information, such as desktops, laptops, tablets, and application systems running on these devices. We will later look at network services, which include network devices, network systems, and other supporting systems. We will also look at Internet technologies, which will include web technologies, social media, and other Internet-related services.

The dependence on Internet services has grown such that we can no longer do away with such services as individuals, businesses, and public enterprises.

These three areas (information access, network services, and Internet technologies) will generally give us a good coverage of technologies used in an enterprise.

Information Access

Fifteen to twenty years ago, accessing information for personal or business use was mainly through personal computers. Today information is accessed using a variety of computing devices. In this section, we shall review various tools and different ways used to access information in an enterprise.

a) Workstations

Personal computers and laptops are some of the common devices which are used to access information in offices and homes. Other devices which are used to access information include notebooks, tablets, iPads, and smartphones. Terminals with or without processing power are also used as workstations in offices. Where high-powered computing is required, users may make use of workstations connected to minicomputers, mainframe or supercomputers. This is common in research institutions requiring high-powered computing services. Workstations normally would consist of monitors, keyboards, mouse, cameras (i.e. webcams), printers, scanners, and other forms of input and output devices.

IS auditors should take notice of the type of workstations used in the IT environment so that they are able to assess risks involved in using these devices. Use of smartphones, which are connected to enterprise networks, is a common feature nowadays. The phones are used to access enterprise information and, in many cases, access enterprise systems via customised networks or the Internet. We also have noticed the introduction of wearable devices which are used to communicate with office systems via Bluetooth for example. All these devices introduce different risks when used to connect to office networks.

The benefits of using workstations are that they provide us with the ability to capture large volumes of data, access to data in remote locations through networks, and the Internet. We can also use our workstations to process complex data either independently as a stand-alone workstation or through other bigger computers, such as mainframes and supercomputers.

The IS auditor should understand the role of audit objectives and how they are developed. Audit objectives are normally determined by management or the department concerned and may vary in content depending on business requirements. Below in figure 4.1 are some generic audit objectives which can be considered when auditing workstations:

#	Audit Objective	Environment
1	Security of the workstations (physical and logical)	Workstation
2	Availability of antivirus and antimalware software	Workstation
3	Access controls using user account and password	Workstation

4	Hardening of security on the workstation operating system	Workstation
5	Availability of supported version of operating system on workstations	Workstation
6	Secure connectivity to network devices such as servers, printers, and Internet	Workstation
7	Security for wireless connections	Workstation
8	Determine approved application systems on workstation	Workstation
9	Availability of patches to update workstation OS software	Workstation
10	Protection of data on the workstation	Workstation

Figure 4.1 Workstation Audit Objectives

b) Operating Systems

Workstations are operated and controlled by operating system software such as Windows, Android, iOS, Linux, BlackBerry, and Ubuntu. Operating system software are powerful systems not only found on computers but on all computing devices, including modern devices which we use in our everyday life such as cameras, smartphones, wearable devices such as smart glasses and wristwatches. Operating systems perform various functions on workstations and facilitate the use of application systems, such as office productivity tools. Operating systems are also used to enable communication with other computers on networks and the Internet.

In order to ensure that operating systems operate as expected, they should be properly configured and meet workstation configuration standards as determined by the enterprise. The IS audit team can use a compliance checklist to test whether the workstation operating system meets the required workstation configuration standards.

Auditing operating systems provides us with an assurance that the computers being used provide a secure environment. IS auditors should review various aspects of the operating system, which include the following audit objectives:

1) all ports not in use should be closed
2) workstation wireless adapters should be disabled on sensitive segments of the network
3) only latest versions of operating system should be installed on workstations
4) operating systems should be security hardened on all workstations.

An audit may specifically focus on auditing an operating system only instead of all software on the workstation. In this case, the IS audit team might look at specific audit objectives relating to the operating system. There are various types of operating systems and operating on different devices. The focus of a particular operating system audit will depend on business and usage requirements.

c) Application Systems

Application systems have been included on the list of technologies because they are commonly used in office environments to process data and generate information. Application systems are also used to carry out specific functions. Common uses in enterprises include automation of customer relations management, human resources, finance, and procurement. These application systems can be used as stand-alone application system or integrated with other office systems.

Office productivity application systems are also common in enterprises and are used to support our everyday activities, such as sending emails, making calculations, storing data, publishing reports and newsletters, making presentations, among many other activities. Because a lot of company data is generated and stored using these tools, the IS auditor should take interest in how data is protected and stored.

Vendors are also able to provide software as a service (SaaS). This type of use of software has become popular as users do not need to install software on their computers. This is a software distribution model were application systems are hosted by a service provider and made available to customers. Different types of software can be accessed online.

On the top end, there are enterprise resource planning systems (ERP), which are integrated systems used across the enterprise. All functions in the enterprise would have a module which is used to input and access data. The benefit of ERP systems is that data is only entered once and can be used by all modules in the ERP system. For example, if the administration department placed a request for computers, the same data will be processed and used to issue a purchase order by the procurement department and to make payment by the finance department. The audit function will also use the same data to review transactions made during the financial year.

The systems implemented could be end to end and across the entire enterprise. This raises the need to ensure that data is protected and appropriate controls are implemented throughout the ERP system. It is the responsibility of the IS auditor to ensure that these controls are regularly reviewed and that management is given an assurance that they are properly designed, effective, and operating according to defined business rules.

The IS audit team might look at various audit objectives in order to assess the proper functioning of application systems and effectiveness of controls. Audit objectives for application systems might include assessing:

1) effectiveness of access controls
2) recovery of data
3) availability of input controls
4) audit logging
5) controls during data transfer
6) availability of output controls
7) database controls
8) processing controls
9) security controls
10) communication controls.

d) Antivirus and Antimalware Systems

Workstations which we use to access and process data are vulnerable to various threats, including viruses and malware. In order to provide effective protection from such threats, enterprises do implement antivirus protection on workstations. The antivirus systems can be either stand-alone or centrally managed. There are many types of virus-protection software on the market. Each one of them is able to protect workstations to various degrees, and users might find that some antivirus tools are more effective than others. The effectiveness of antivirus software also depends how the virus-protection system is administered and configured.

Virus definition files are used by antivirus systems to detect viruses. A virus definition file contains a list of known viruses and should be updated often to be current. How often virus definition files are updated depends on the requirements of a particular enterprise. In many enterprises, virus definitions are updated on a daily basis or as they are made available by the vendors.

User awareness is key to the success of any antivirus solution. Users should be trained to avoid situations which may lead to their workstations being infected. Viruses can be devastating and can take some time to cure if there is a network-wide infection. For example, it is important that users should:

1) not download files from unknown sources
2) scan their PCs regularly
3) update virus definitions
4) avoid using disk drives from unknown sources
5) scan drives and other sources of data before use

6) ensure automatic scanning of incoming and outgoing emails.

The benefits of using antivirus protection software are many. It is important that users appreciate the use of antivirus software. Deliberate training programs should be implemented in order to ensure that users are able to use the antivirus software effectively.

Most enterprises have put in place policies and procedures regarding implementation of antivirus protection. IS auditors can use these policies and procedures to assess implementation and effectiveness of virus-protection systems. The audit objectives for conducting IS audits for antivirus protection systems would include:

1) availability of antivirus policies and procedures
2) evidence of user awareness training
3) statistics on infection incidents
4) status on updating virus definitions
5) general effectiveness of the antivirus solution.

e) Web Access

Access to information can also be made possible by using web applications. Web access tools have become popular nowadays, as they are easier and more flexible to use. Most enterprises offer services to customers via the Internet and users are required to input or access data using web browsers, such as Internet Explorer, Mozilla, Chrome, Firefox, Opera, Safari, and many other similar applications.

Web application systems have many uses which include e-banking, webmail, online shopping, e-learning, blogs, and social media, such as Twitter, Facebook, and LinkedIn. Users have found the use of web applications easy to use, hence the increase in popularity. Web applications also enable high-content and real-time communication with users. We have also seen the use of document and video-sharing among users of web applications. Examples include use of YouTube, Skype, and Instagram.

There are many security risks arising from using web applications as they are vulnerable to various attacks. Due to the nature of activities which are conducted on the Internet, many hackers have been attacking web servers in order to access data or corrupt data stored on these commercial and public systems. In many cases, hackers have tried to access web servers for financial gain.

The major weakness of web applications includes the use of Internet traffic through port 80, which is normally open to allow Internet traffic. It is recommended to use the secure https when communicating with servers. Configuration of web servers not to allow certain types of data validations and data capture methods is an important web security procedure.

IS auditors should assess risks related to web application systems very often because Internet technologies are always changing and new risk exposures are being discovered every time. IS audit teams are required to review audit objectives developed by the enterprise and provide appropriate comments and recommendations. Some of the audit objectives which the audit team might be given to perform an audit include:

1) ensuring monitoring of web servers
2) web server configuration should be according to approved standards

3) unused services on the web server should be disabled
4) using malware filter on web server.

f) Communication Tools

In most enterprises, the predominant form of communication is by email. There are various software tools which are used to facilitate email communication. Some enterprises prefer to use email applications such as Microsoft Outlook and Mozilla Thunderbird. It is also common to find use of web-based email systems such as Gmail, Yahoo, and Outlook web access. A lot of corporate information is sent and received using emails. Email communication should be protected as it forms a critical part of a company's data silos. Other forms of communication in an office environment include social media blogs, SMS, and other internal communication tools. The Internet, which we will discuss later in this chapter, is an important catalyst to email communication in the office and between enterprises.

Due to the importance of email communication and the sensitivity of information which is generated and used by businesses, it is essential that IS auditors recognise the need to protect this information. Most enterprises have put in place measures of protecting emails generated by businesses for future reference or record. Most of these emails and other forms of communication are backed up from servers and workstations and stored on backup storage media.

The IS auditor should ensure that communication data is properly backed up and can be accessed when needed. Communication data is equally important just as data generated through other business and financial transactions. When requested to carry out an audit, the following are some of the audit objectives the IS auditor might be given by management:

1) ensure recovery of lost email data
2) security of email servers
3) observance of personal privacy
4) implementation of access controls to protect email communication
5) securing of SMS, blogs, social media, and other non-email data
6) compliance with email policies
7) acceptable use of communication tools such as webmail
8) integration of email with other forms of communication
9) compliance with email communication policies and regulations.

g) Input Systems and Output Systems

There are various input and output systems which are used to capture and view data on computer systems. Developments in technology have brought about new tools which are now used to capture and access information.

In addition to traditional input systems such as keyboards, monitors, scanners, and mouse, other forms of input systems have been introduced in office environments and have changed the way we capture data. Touch screens are now widely used for capturing data. Special cameras are also used to capture real-time data and convert it into human understandable information in the form of reports and graphs. This information is captured without human intervention. Sensors can also be used as monitoring devices as they are able to report on various production processes, quality control, and status of production equipment.

Advancements in system integration have enabled automation of data input from one system to the other with limited or no human intervention. This has made capturing of data very easy and also provided the capability to capture large volumes of data.

Output systems have also undergone transformation in the way we access information with the introduction of new technologies. Output systems can be used to produce information using touch screens and converting voice output into text and vice versa. Using new technologies, output can also be produced using automated reports, which is immediately used as input into other systems.

Integrated systems are also able to accept output from other systems. Output from one system may be input for another system. This is now common in most integrated systems as it ensures efficiency in data capture and also accuracy of input. Most enterprises rely on the use of complex and feature-rich ERP systems with enhanced system integration features.

The benefits of new input and output systems are efficiency, speed, and accuracy. New technologies, despite the benefits, have brought about new risks to the enterprise. IS auditors need to ensure that possible risks are identified and recommend to management effective ways of mitigating these risks.

The audit objectives for auditing input and output systems may include testing:

1) existence of field input validation
2) system-to-system data transfer controls
3) compliance with personal privacy regulations
4) existence of access controls for input and output systems
5) integration controls and procedures
6) data-conversion controls
7) web page input controls
8) web page output controls.

h) Processing Systems

Processing systems can be described in both hardware and software terms. Different classes of computer systems such as supercomputers, mainframe computers, minicomputers, microcomputers, and other smaller systems have different types and sizes of processors with varying processing capacities. Processing power is ever on the increase with advancement in technologies. What was the most powerful microcomputer twenty years ago has today the same processing power as the smartphone.

Speed, processing power, and ability to handle complex programs and data usually determine which class of computer system to use. Information processing requirements in medium to large enterprises would require the use of servers and minicomputers to handle data processing requirements. Very large companies would use mainframe computers. Research institutions and other larger enterprises would require the use of supercomputers to process large volumes of data (big data) and complex high-end database systems.

Servers, mini and mainframe computers use different operating systems which vary in complexity and processing capacity. Servers use operating systems, such as Windows, Unix, and Linux operating system. Minicomputers would also use generic operating systems as well as proprietary systems which are common on mainframe computers.

Some application and database systems are built specifically for certain types of processors. For example, because of the need to process complex computations in a research study, special purpose-built applications and databases can be used on mainframe or supercomputers.

IS auditors will need to look at various factors when auditing processing systems. Generally the focus of the audit would be on the operating systems. Hardware requirements can also form part of the audit if the objective is to test whether the hardware specifications meet the required processing requirements.

i) Storage Devices

There are various types of storage devices which are used to store data on our laptops, tablets, and servers. All the terabytes of data generated by enterprises are held on storage media. It is important that these storage devices are secured and data is protected. Enterprises go a long mile just to ensure that data is protected by providing a correct environment for the storage devices.

Disk storage is a common and widely used storage media. Disk storage comes in various sizes from as little as one gigabyte on a flash disk to huge disks which can store millions of gigabytes of data. Disk storage uses magnetic material to store data and wears off with usage. Exposure to hostile environments can also damage disks.

Tape storage is another type of storage media which is used to store data and commonly used to store backup data. The use of tape storage devices have reduced as most enterprises are moving to disk media, which is more efficient in recording and reading data.

IS auditors should ensure that storage devices are kept in secure places and appropriate environments. Environment controls are very important in ensuring that the devices can be used for a long time and are not easily damaged. Storage manufacturers recommend that storage devices should be replaced after a specified period of use, such as a three years or less. Even if you loved your disk storage device, you will eventually be forced to replace it due to technological changes and advancement.

IS auditors will use audit objectives developed by management to assess various storage devices in use in the enterprise. Management should ensure that storage devices are properly secured and data is protected. Auditors will also be required to ensure that performance of storage devices is according to recommended specifications. Storage devices should not be a bottleneck in the accessing and processing of data. It is the role of the IS auditor that management is advised appropriately on the best storage technologies for the enterprise.

j) Database Systems

Database systems are used to store data captured using application systems or data collected from other applications and databases. Database systems make the work of data analysts easier as they are able to carry out complex data manipulation to produce various performance reports. Databases can handle large amounts of business data which enterprises produce during the course of business.

Information managers use data sitting on company silos to identify various activities, such as sales performance, profitability, competitiveness, and even identify cases of fraud and revenue leakages.

Data analytics is one of the major uses of data sitting on databases. IS auditors make use of data analysis software such as ACL, IDEA, SAS, even Excel to conduct investigations, clean up data, and discover data input errors. Data sitting on databases can also be used for business intelligence such as transforming raw data into meaningful information, which can be used for business decision-making.

There are various database systems such as Microsoft SQL 2014, IBM DB2, Oracle 12c, and SAP HANA developed for commercial use. There are also open-source databases, which are in use in many enterprises such as MySQL, Apache Derby, and SQLite.

IS auditors have a very important role to play in ensuring that data integrity is maintained on databases. This can be done through regular audits of database systems. IS audits include but are not limited to testing data integrity, data security, data privacy, database system controls, and data recovery procedures.

k) Big Data

Big data is a new and growing phenomenon with a great impact on the way we do business and on the type of information which is made available for decision-making by business executives. Big data involves very large volumes of data which are generated by enterprises as single, vertically or horizontally integrated enterprises. The size of data has become so large that our current database systems and applications have challenges in processing the data. Using big data, business managers are able to investigate data relationships, make comparisons, and identify correlations. Big data holds a lot of secrets for the enterprise which can be discovered through data analytics. Good examples include investigating increasing operational costs, market trends, performance levels, and revenue leakages.

Enterprises generate millions of megabytes of data per day, which are stored on enterprise data silos. The challenge is that this data is growing every day, and storing it has become a big issue. The bigger challenge is how to process this data as it requires superfast computers and large storage. Currently, in order to process such large volumes of data, enterprises need many computer systems to work together. A solution has to be found on how this data can be stored and processed. Database developers are investing large sums of money in new database technologies which can handle big data more efficiently.

The benefits of big data are that managers are able to discover hidden information relating to how the business is being run. Big data using superfast computers can enable managers and researchers to figure out what type of products would interest customers in the future. Big data is seen as the next frontier of sources of competition among enterprises and an enabler of productivity and innovation.

With the coming of big data, companies can evaluate different options and make important business decisions especially those which could not be made due to limited information or processing capacity. Big data has opened up a new world of opportunities, which will not only affect businesses but also researches in discovering new treatments for diseases, finding answers to the worlds of unknowns in the universe, and climate change.

IS auditors have a major challenge of working with big data as they have to find better processing capacity. Big data will also create better opportunities of conducting investigations and coming up with relevant findings, conclusions, and recommendations.

Network Services

In today's information age and advanced use of computer systems, we have become so depended on the use of data and information sitting on enterprise databases. In order to access and share this information, we rely on network technologies which are integrated to make networks work. It is important that an IS auditor has a good appreciation of the purpose of computer networks and the various components which make up these networks. The main goal of the IS auditor is to be able to understand audit objectives of the various network devices and systems found in an IT environment.

a) Computer Networks

The purpose of networks is to enable accessing and sharing of data and information among users in an enterprise. Networks are also used to share devices and systems, such as servers, storage, printers, photocopies, telephone systems, Internet bandwidth, and many other devices commonly used in an office.

There are different types of networks which can be used to access various resources. Local area networks (LAN) are used to connect computers and other associated devices within an office environment. A LAN could be used by a few users to thousands of users in an office complex. A metropolitan area network (MAN) would be set up where users are spread over various offices in a town or city. Office LANs in a city or town can be linked up to form a MAN. On a larger scale where an enterprise has branch offices over long distances, such as intercity or across countries, such networks are referred to as wide area networks (WAN).

Different types of network technologies are used to connect computers, LANs, MANs, and WANs. In offices, you will come across Ethernet cables which have speed ranging from 100 mbps to 1,000 mbps. These are usually copper cables which link computers and network servers via Ethernet ports.

Fibre optic cables, which consist of glass strands and use light to transmit data, are also used to form LANs and larger networks such as MANs and WANs. Fibre networks are faster than Ethernet networks in terms of data speeds. Data transfer speed of 1 mbps or more are possible on fibre networks.

Wireless technologies can also be used to implement networks such as LANs or MANs. Wireless networks use radio technologies such as Wi-Fi. Wireless technologies can also be used to connect office equipment such as printers, scanners, and photocopies.

Enterprises should take interest in ensuring that networks are secured using various security technologies because of the important function networks serve. Key among the various functions is the central storage of data and also the ability to share resources among many users. We will review in detail issues relating to network security in chapter 7.

IS auditors should review the network infrastructure in order to ensure that network resources are protected from both internal and external threats. Audit objectives for auditing networks are many, and we will review these objectives below by looking at individual network devices which are used to design and develop computer networks.

b) Network Firewalls

Firewalls are used to protect internal enterprise resources, such as data, information, and servers, from external threats. There are thousands of hackers out there waiting for an opportunity to exploit vulnerabilities on firewalls. Firewalls play a very important role in securing enterprise networks. Firewalls can be hardware-based or software-based running on a computer server.

The way a firewall is configured also plays an important role of how it secures the internal network. IS auditors who are specialised in firewall installations would review firewall configuration either using command- or web-based versions. Firewall vendors would normally develop configuration standards which enterprises can adopt or customise default configurations by including internally developed firewall policies.

There are different audit objectives which can be used to audit firewalls. Note that there are also personal firewalls on personal computers which are designed to protect a computer system from both internal and external threats.

Management might request an IS auditor to audit both parameter and personal firewalls. The following are some of the audit objectives which may be used to audit firewalls:

1) test the effectiveness of firewall policies
2) review the firewall configuration and determine whether the firewall was configured according to enterprise-firewall policies
3) check for unused open ports on firewalls
4) test if the firewall is regularly monitored
5) test if IT management does regularly receive reports on performance of firewalls
6) test if there are attempts to hack into the internal network using firewall-generated data.

c) Network Routers

Network routers are used to route traffic from internal sources to outside destinations and vice versa. Routers also are used to route traffic between various computers within an internal network. Enterprises implement either hardware or software routers. Hardware routers are quite common in many enterprises such as CISCO routers.

Routers can be used to perform many other networks functions apart from its core function of routing traffic. In smaller enterprises where traffic is light, routers are used to perform DHCP functions, provide DNS services, and segmenting the network.

Routers also differ in size and capacity. In bigger enterprises where traffic is heavy, high-capacity routers are used which are able to handle heavy traffic. In some enterprises, IS auditors will find more than one router and each performing a specific function or for load balancing.

Typically, you will find routers handling internal traffic and other routers handling external traffic. Monitoring tools can be installed to monitor traffic on routers.

Audit objectives for routers might include reviewing:

1. router configuration in order to determine if it is properly configured
2. router security configuration
3. router traffic and load
4. router performance
5. router specifications versus planned standards
6. router installations and connections.

d) Network Switches

Network switches are used to link devices on a network using ports available on a switch. Switches may have 12, 24, 36, or more Ethernet ports on which computers and other network devices are plugged. Switches act as a link between devices which are installed on the network. Some network switches are configured to also perform routing of traffic on the internal network and also perform intelligent decision-making when routing traffic.

Depending on traffic and demand on internal bandwidth, IT management might require higher specification network switches. For example, memory and processing capacity might be a bottleneck on a switch such that IT management might request that higher memory be installed on the switch or upgrade switches to have higher capacity processors. This could also mean replacing the old switches with new high-capacity switches.

Management should ensure that routers provide high performance on the network. Management might require

IS auditors to review performance of switches, security of switches, configuration, and efficient setup of VLANs.

e) Network Servers

Network servers are used to provide shared network resources to users. The common uses of network servers are to provide storage and access to centrally stored data and information. There are many other functions of network servers.

Servers can also be used to run application systems accessed by thousands, if not millions, of customers and internal users. Network servers can also be used to run printing services, databases, backup services, network monitoring services, and centralised authentication of users.

Network servers have changed the way companies provide services to customers. Most services today are automated such that there is little interaction between customers and internal company staff. Take for example, if you are a customer on Amazon.com, you would browse the web portal, select a product you want, and make an order. You will receive your product upon payment within a few days. All this will be done by interacting with a web application running on servers with no or limited interaction with customer support staff.

Since network servers play such a critical role on our networks, IS auditors are often called upon to check performance of these servers. Auditors may be required to perform the following tests:

1. review that servers are properly configured
2. check that servers are regularly monitored
3. check maintenance of servers

4. test compliance with internal policies and procedures
5. test compliance with server change management
6. test data integrity and access controls
7. ensure server applications and operating systems are up to date
8. ensure security hardening of server operating systems.

f) Modems

There are various types of modems which are used on the network infrastructure. Modems are normally used to provide connectivity to other networks or systems. For example digital subscriber line (DSL) modems are used to connect enterprises to Internet service providers or to connect to other office networks, such as a branch office. Most modems in use today are digital modems unlike a few years ago when we had analogue modems which were used to provide connectivity.

New developments in connectivity technology have seen the deployment of dongles, which are used to connect computers to the Internet and office networks through virtual private network (VPN) connections. Phone SIM cards are used on dongles to connect to service providers, other corporate networks, or the Internet.

Modems and dongles pose a number of security challenges if used on a corporate network. Many times you will find that the use of these dongles has not been authorised for use on corporate networks by management. It is common to find users connecting to both the unsecure external network using dongles and, at the same time, connecting to the secure local network using Ethernet connections or other technologies. This exposes the internal network to possible hacking from unauthorised users on the unsecure external network.

IS auditors should ensure that modems are configured properly and are compliant with standard configurations approved by management.

g) Telephone Systems

It is important to understand why enterprises are integrating telephone systems into the corporate network infrastructure. One reason of course is that IP telephone systems are more efficient than ordinary telephone systems. The other reason is to take advantage of the many good features of IP telephone systems, which include storing telephone data on company storage. The enterprise might require that customers' telephone records are kept for legal reasons, and storing such data in digital format is more efficient in terms of both storage space and retrieval.

Mobile phone systems are nowadays also integrated into corporate telephone networks in order to ensure quick and easy communication across networks. Data generated on mobile phones, in addition to voice data, include SMS, emails, and social media records, such as Facebook and Twitter data.

Data generated using telephone systems need to be protected as it is important corporate data. IS auditors need to ensure that telephone data and supporting systems are protected and that, in the event of an incident, the data can be recovered.

Digital telephone systems can also be attacked by viruses and hackers. Necessary protection needs to be provided in order to secure telephone systems. Social engineering is also one possible attack which enterprises need to be aware of and use IS auditors to ensure that necessary policies and procedures are in place and supported by user awareness programs.

h) CCTV

Closed-circuit television (CCTV) has grown in importance and use as it provides tools for monitoring activities in the enterprise. The records obtained can be used as evidence in a court of law in the event that there is fraud or theft. Use of CCTV has been on the increase, and many enterprises have deployed CCTV in their environments. In some countries, it is a legal requirement to install CCTV in key and sensitive areas.

The use of dummy CCTV (non-active) is also permissible in some jurisdictions. Such installations are used as decoy to keep away intruders and potential theft. Key security personnel and management should be made aware of this deployment to avoid misunderstanding.

Data collected and stored from CCTV should be stored for a specific duration in backup storage where it can easily be retrieved for use. In some countries, there are legal requirements for CCTV data to be stored for more than seven years. CCTV technology has also improved over the years such that large volumes of data can be stored in digital format and can be quickly retrieved from storage.

There are many audit objectives which can be used to review CCTV infrastructure. Some of the audit objectives include:

1. regular review of CCTV data
2. application of access controls to CCTV data
3. implementation of security procedures for CCTV
4. safe and secure storage of CCTV data
5. compliance with legal requirements.

i) Date Centres

Data centres are areas in an enterprise which are used to locate network servers, database servers, application system servers, and network equipment, such as routers, firewalls, and switches. Data centres are the heart of enterprises which are highly dependent on the use of IT systems. In a highly automated enterprise, most business processes are carried out using application systems located in data centres. Because of this critical role, data centres are given high priority security. IS auditors are often called in to review compliance with security procedures at data centres in order to ensure maximum application of security measures.

There are a number of other considerations which the IS auditor should take into account when auditing data centres, such as data centre environmental controls, access to the data centre, power supply, and air conditioning.

Internet Technologies

The growth and use of the Internet has greatly influenced the way enterprises operate. Most of our activities both in the office and our own personal situations are nowadays dependent on the Internet in many ways. How we communicate and access information is mostly dependent on the Internet as well. Enterprises conduct most of their business using the Internet.

There is no sizable enterprise with geographically dispersed customers today which does not use email to communicate.

a) The Internet

The Internet is a large public network with millions of users providing or receiving various types of services. The Internet has grown so large that it produces millions of megabytes per day. The Internet consists of the World Wide Web, which we use to host websites, the email systems, which we are so dependent on to send and receive emails, and the file transfer protocol, which we use to download files and documents for personal or business use.

Enterprises use the Internet to conduct business and also communicate with customers and business partners. Many financial transactions are conducted on the Internet by enterprises around the world. Customers also purchase various types of goods and services on the Internet. Not all Internet users have good intentions. Others are there to defraud enterprises or hack into their systems in order to steal corporate data. Over the years, we have seen how vulnerable Internet users are with many large enterprises having their customer data, such as credit card information, exposed to the public.

Enterprises are always investigating new ways of protecting their resources from threats which exist by connecting to the Internet. Various types of security measures are implemented in order to secure company resources from hackers on the Internet. Security companies have developed different types of security software just dedicated to protecting IT systems.

The IS auditor has a very important role of ensuring that company resources are protected from threats which exist on the Internet. IS auditors are often required to carry out reviews based on various audit objectives such as:

1. protection of users and enterprises from hackers
2. protection of computer systems from viruses and malware
3. provision of firewall protection
4. provision of intrusion detection
5. provision of intrusion prevention
6. secure routing of Internet traffic
7. controlled Internet access in the office
8. controlled use of web applications
9. protection of email systems.

b) Cloud Computing

Cloud computing is basically the use of remote servers to host, administer, and process data. The service is provided by cloud service providers using the Internet. Cloud services include hosting application systems, data, and recovery services. Cloud services have become popular with many enterprises as they relieve the enterprise from administering and managing locally hosted application systems, data, and servers. The overall running costs are much lower because most of the key IT services are provided by cloud service providers.

Some enterprises point to security and privacy issues as reasons why they are reluctant to use cloud services. There are many examples of breaches of security littered everywhere, such as large customer databases being hacked into. But these security weaknesses should not definitely deter enterprises from using cloud computing services, which are playing a big role in ensuring that enterprises provide high-quality services to their customers.

Major considerations for the auditor include:

1. security of data
2. availability of services
3. access controls to application systems
4. mobility of users
5. recovery of data and application systems
6. service-level agreement with service providers.

c) Social Media

Social media is the interaction of users on the Internet to create, share, and communicate using social media sites and applications. Virtual groups are normally created and used as a base for social communication. Membership to these virtual groups is based on common interest. Business enterprises have opened accounts on social media sites to promote their businesses, market their products, or merely establishing their presence on social media sites. It is common to see individuals creating accounts and invite friends with common interests to follow them. Common examples of social media sites include Facebook and Twitter.

There are various ways in which social media is conducted such as through the use of Internet forums, blogs, podcasts, wikis, etc. Mobile social media has seen fast growth due to the use of mobile phones. Examples of mobile social media sites also include sites such as Facebook, WhatsApp, and Twitter. Because mobile social media provides instant communication, most users prefer to use such media. There are many other social media sites in use worldwide but vary in popularity and focus.

Social media have grown in usage and popularity worldwide such that it is now part of our lives just like mobile phones have changed the way we communicate. Actually the drive on the growth of social media has been mobile phones.

Because businesses are also generating data on social media, enterprises should protect this business data and store it for current and future use. Audit objectives would include security of data, access to data, risk to data, securing web applications, and protection of social media communities.

d) Web Portals

Web portals are web pages or websites dedicated to providing specific information to users or customers. Web portals would have information extracted from company databases or intranets. Web portals can be used to provide a standard set of data such as dashboards to systems administrators monitoring IT systems or customers interested in specific product information. Web portals serve various purposes, and because they use corporate data in many cases, it is important that this data is protected. Some enterprises provide read only access to data without features for interacting with users. Where user interaction is required, access to data is a key consideration. Measures should be put in place to ensure that access to data is controlled.

Web portals and websites are often attacked by hackers in order to bring down the sites for personal or commercial reasons. The IS auditor has an important task of making sure that web developers include all necessary controls and security features in order to protect web portals. The IS auditor should review the web portals with a view of finding out if they are compliant with web portal security and controls.

e) Cybersecurity

Cybersecurity is the protection of IT systems from deliberate or intentional destruction or modifications. IT systems need to be protected from viruses and hackers both internal and external to the enterprise such as the Internet. Most cybersecurity challenges originate from the use of the Internet. Different measures are usually put in place to protect both IT systems and data which is generated when using IT systems.

Enterprises implement cybersecurity based on security standards or frameworks. A common standard used for implementing information security is ISO 27001, and IS auditors should have a good understanding of this standard in order to perform effective audits.

Use of access controls is one action of ensuring that data and systems are protected. Users who are authorised to access systems are given user rights on a need-to-know basis. Rights are usually based on job description and other necessary job roles.

Various technologies are used to protect IT systems such that many enterprises employ staff dedicated to providing security services such as implementing and managing security systems.

Enterprises should always be prepared to recover from incidents. Being prepared to adequately handle incidents is part of cybersecurity, and enterprises are required to do so by regulation or internally developed policies. IS auditors should review cybersecurity regularly in order to ensure that the enterprise is protected. Auditors play a critical role and should always provide advisory services to management on security matters.

f) E-commerce

E-commerce is the buying and selling of goods and services on the Internet or other computer networks. E-commerce is a very big industry as many enterprises have moved to using e-commerce as it is more efficient and less costly to conduct business. Enterprises conduct their business using websites or portals which customers use to view and place orders for the goods and services they want.

E-commerce, through the Internet, has enabled enterprises worldwide to sell their products on the international market. This was not possible before e-commerce became a reality. E-commerce generates a lot of data, and transactions worth billions of dollars are conducted using this platform. Because of the many transactions being conducted through e-commerce and high financial value, the industry has also attracted hackers and other illegal business enterprises that often attack legitimate sites and steal money and data.

IS auditors have an important role in protecting e-commerce operations by regularly reviewing data security and protection of e-commerce infrastructure. IS auditors might be required to review the following areas when auditing e-commerce infrastructure:

1. security for e-commerce sites
2. protection of clients' transactions
3. privacy for clients' personal data
4. identification of potential threats
5. identification of e-commerce business risks.

g) Teleworking

Teleworking is a concept where employees work from home or a different location using different types of technologies. Many teleworkers are part-time workers although you will find in some countries full-time employees working as teleworkers part of their working days. Teleworking is common for call centre workers, IT staff, writers, and other professionals whose job does not require physically commuting to a central workplace.

In order to telework, an employee will be required to use communication technologies which will facilitate such work. An example would be a software developer who would work from home and submit work via email or web portals. The developer can use facilities at his workplace to test software modules he has developed using remotely hosted servers. Teleworkers, in such a case, would require connectivity linking him to the office network. Possible links would be via telephone lines, fibre links, or satellite. The advent of the Internet has changed the way many professionals work as it has provided most of the resources teleworkers need to use.

The IS auditor should take into consideration the resource requirements for such a workforce. Security is one of the major issues which need to be considered as the employee may expose company data to unauthorised users. The IS auditor should also look at security controls required to establish connectivity with teleworkers and confidentiality agreements between the company and teleworkers.

h) E-Learning

E-learning is about the use of IT systems to deliver training. E-learning has grown in usage such that a large number of university and college courses are now delivered using e-learning. Distance learning is now conducted using e-learning as it is more efficient and facilitates quick communications between the learners and faculty.

Most e-learning courses are delivered using the Internet. Enterprises also use e-learning systems to deliver training within their corporate walls using internal networks. Learners can register for courses via university or college web portals and access courses via the Internet. Courses are delivered using e-learning systems which manage the course delivery process from delivery of training, interactions with faculty, course assignments, and examinations. Different types of media are used during course delivery, which includes video, text, audio, animations, and live lectures delivered by professors around the world.

The audit objectives which may be given to an IS auditor might include the following:

1. security of course assessments and examinations
2. secure course platforms
3. secure registration systems
4. protected payment systems
5. use of efficient network systems and availability of sufficient Internet bandwidth.

i) Business-to-Business Systems

Business-to-business refers to the conduct of business transactions between enterprises. This could be between manufacturers and distributors or wholesalers or retailers. Most businesses have taken advantage of these business relationships through the use of technology and the Internet.

In order to ensure efficient communication and delivery systems between enterprises (i.e. manufacturer and distributor), integrated IT systems are used. Automated production systems can be designed such that they produce goods ordered by the distributor and shipped to the right warehouses and onward to retailers with minimum interventions. Raw materials would be ordered through B2B transactions from multiple suppliers. The suppliers provide raw materials according to goods ordered by distributors. B2B systems are efficient in that there are no excess raw materials ordered and no excess stock in the manufacturer's warehouse.

Such systems are complex and require precision in systems interaction. Highly automated and sophisticated systems are required to manage such processes. IS auditors are required to regularly check maintenance of such systems to ensure that production is not disrupted. The IS auditors also should ensure that transactions between businesses are conducted in a secure and transparent manner in order to ensure a continuous flow of services and production.

j) Search Engines

Search engines are software tools which are used on the Internet to search for information required by users. Search engines are advanced tools which are able to search information silos on the Internet and provide the required results. There are many search engines which are used to access information from the Internet. There are commonly used search tools such as Google, Bing, and Yahoo. There are several other powerful search tools available for use, and most of them are free. Each of these search engines are able to search for information using different word combinations and even more complex search requests.

The Internet has made the life of a researcher and learner much easier as they are now able to find most of the information they need within a short time. The new challenge for the researcher and learner is trying to find information required from a vast array of information provided by search engines.

Businesses also make use of these search engines to look for business information and also to collaborate and validate information they have on competitors, for example. Not all the information you find on the Internet is factually correct. Some of the information may be out of date, or the conclusion made in the documents was based on wrong analysis. The IS auditor has to ensure that enterprises have policies and procedures in place on how such information is collected and used for producing company reports or research results. Incorrect data will often result into incorrect information.

The technologies we have reviewed in this chapter are only a small percentage of what the IS auditor is expected to know, but the information provided will help as a starting point. The IS auditor can use the Internet and other sources to investigate technologies not covered in this chapter. What is important is being able to understand what the technology being researched is all about and what the possible audit objectives could be so that the IS auditor can understand how to formulate appropriate conclusions and recommendations which are directly linked to the audit objectives.

CHAPTER 5

IT Governance

Overview

One notable role of the IS auditor among others is to assess whether IT governance in an enterprise has been implemented properly, is working, and is contributing to the success of the enterprise. The IS auditor is also a professional person in the enterprise charged with adding value to the enterprise by providing effective IT assurance services. A good understanding of IT governance and its implementation by the IS auditor is essential in order to ensure that IT enables enhanced performance of the enterprise. In this chapter, we shall review how IT governance is implemented in an enterprise and the process of performing IT governance audits.

ISACA defines IT governance as 'IT governance is the responsibility of the board of directors and executive management. It is an integral part of enterprise governance and consists of the leadership and organisational structures and processes that ensure that the enterprise's IT sustains and extends the enterprise's strategies and objectives.'

IT governance is also about how we use and manage information systems, technology, communication, business, and other processes related to usage of IT resources in the enterprise. High dependence on IT means that IT resources need to be used efficiently and prudently. The use of IT has brought about many benefits to enterprises and has had an impact throughout all levels of an enterprise. It is therefore important that consideration should be given to proper governance of IT in order to achieve organizational goals.

IT governance is also of concern to many other stakeholders and not just IT professionals. If IT governance has to be effective, the involvement of key stakeholders is required. In an enterprise stakeholder such as shareholders, the board, senior management, business partners, IT suppliers, and IS auditors need to be concerned with IT governance. IT governance is part of corporate governance and contributes to the overall implementation of governance in an enterprise.

Many enterprises that have implemented IT governance have experienced many benefits which include value addition to the business, protection of IT resources, effective mitigation of risk, and efficient use of human resources. Through the use of IT, many enterprises have been able to add value by introduction of new business processes, identification of revenue leakages, and in many cases, introduction of new and efficient products.

IT governance is the responsibility of the board of directors and the executive management. However, the role of the board and that of management should be separated and their performance measured using different metrics. The IS auditor should develop and use different performance metrics which can be used to access the contribution of each level to the success of the enterprise.

The purpose of IT governance is to direct IT activities to ensure that IT performance enables achievement of objectives of the enterprise and realization of benefits. In order to achieve high performance and good results, IT objectives should be aligned to business objectives. Where IT objectives are not aligned to business objectives, the result would be having IT operating and pulling in one direction and the business pulling in a different direction. One of the roles of the board and management is to ensure the two are aligned so that the enterprise is able to perform successfully.

The IS auditor should consider reviewing the effectiveness of the alignment between IT goals and those of the business and assess whether the alignment is effective. It is possible to have a well-designed goal alignment on paper but not implemented. The IS auditor is required to review all activities of the board and management in order to assess that IT objectives are properly aligned to business objectives. The IS auditor can collect data on IT governance activities of the enterprise from many sources especially from members of the board and management.

IS auditors play a significant role in the successful and effective implementation of IT governance in an enterprise. Information systems auditors regularly provide IT assurance services which help to ensure effective implementation and maintenance of IT governance. In order to provide an effective IT assurance service, IS auditors should have a good understanding of IT governance and how it is implemented.

Information systems auditors are best positioned to provide leading best practice recommendations to the board and executive management so that the enterprise can improve the quality and effectiveness of IT governance. The role of the IS audit team is also that of a consultant and that of providing value-addition services.

The other important role of IS auditing is to help ensure compliance with IT governance initiatives. These initiatives could be of concern to various levels in the enterprise. Compliance could be based on a governance framework developed internally by the enterprises or an international IT governance framework developed by professional associations or international standards organisations.

Reporting on IT governance may cross divisional, functional, and departmental boundaries as it applies to all. The best lead team composition for IT governance is where the team members (consisting of senior managers) come from various departments with representation from the board. The team members should represent all functions of the enterprise. Implementation of IT governance should be an end-to-end process and not limited to particular functions.

IT Governance Structure

In order for IT governance to be implemented successfully in an enterprise, it should be part of the enterprise processes and structures of governance. On the onset, an IS auditor would be interested in finding out if these structures and processes do exist and used effectively in the enterprise.

IT governance is a board of directors' initiative, and the board should take ownership of the process by giving guidance and clear expectations of what management should do. In order to ensure that IT governance is part of the board activities, it is important that IT issues are part of the board agenda. The board agenda should not only include IT budget items but all IT management issues which require board guidance.

The board should also ensure that management of IT is regularly addressed at senior management level so that all issues are picked up and, where necessary, escalated to the board for support and approval. If issues are not discussed at this level it is likely that they will never be addressed until a major incident happens.

The board and senior management should ensure that IT performance assessment is regularly conducted and reported to the board. It is only through such reports that the board would be able to appreciate use of IT in the enterprise and get involved in enterprise IT governance.

It is important that the board and management make use of IS audit assurance services so that independent assessments of IT governance are conducted regularly. IS audits can be conducted by IT internal or external auditors focusing on IT performance, compliance, or other areas the board might deem necessary.

The first point of implementing IT governance is to set up a framework that will be used to drive the implementation. The framework will outline clear responsibilities for all involved in implementing IT governance. The framework will also indicate objectives of the framework which will be used by various key stakeholders. The framework can be based on various available IT governance standards, which we will cover later in the chapter.

IT governance needs to be supported by setting up an IT strategy or governance committee. The committee will be responsible for implementing and monitoring IT strategies as determined by the board. The committee will also be a link between the board and management. The IT strategy committee will also be responsible for providing an oversight role over lower-level committees, such as IT project teams and IT management teams.

Information Technology Strategy, Policies, and Procedures

The framework developed for IT governance requires to be supported by IT strategies, policies, and procedures. These strategies and policies will provide further guidance to management on how IT should be implemented so that business objectives can be achieved.

The enterprise's IT strategy will give a general direction as to how IT will be implemented in the enterprise. Management will be responsible for implementing the strategy under the supervision of the board. The IT strategy committee will provide a critical role of ensuring clear communication and interpretation of IT strategies. The IT strategy committee would possibly consist of some members of the board and executive management. The exact composition will depend on the structure and size of the enterprise.

The board and management will develop an IT policy to support the IT strategy. The policy will be used by management to guide operations of IT. An IT policy is developed to cover various areas such as IT operations, information security, IT risk, information systems, and disaster recovery and help desk management. The actual implementation of an IT policy will be carried out by the head of IT function supervised by senior management and supported by specialist IT staff and all users in the enterprise.

IT standards can be used to ensure that the enterprise is using best practice IT strategies and systems. Standards are used to support IT policies and procedures and would have been approved by management prior to implementation.

Procedures support various business processes which have been implemented in the enterprise. Procedures are important in that they enable compliance with business rules and also ensure that the enterprise is not exposed to unnecessary risks. Without procedures, employees may conduct business activities the way they deem fit and expose the enterprise to various risks.

Procedures are often embedded in IT systems, and this ensures that when a business process is being carried out, it is subjected to various controls through a procedure in the system and users are not allowed to ignore the procedures.

The IS auditor has an important role of ensuring that IT governance is successful in an enterprise. The board will regularly require that the IS audit team conducts an audit which will require assessment of IT governance in the enterprise. The IS auditor will be interested in reviewing how the board is involved in IT governance and how it is giving guidance to management. The IS auditor would also like to see how the board is assessing performance of IT and what type of reports they receive from management.

The IS auditor will regularly review IT policies and how they are implemented in order to ascertain their effectiveness. Apart from reviewing how the policies are being implemented, the IS auditor will also test IT operations in order to ascertain if they are compliant with approved policies.

IT governance initiatives cannot succeed without supporting strategies, policies, and procedures. Many enterprises ensure that implementation and operation of strategies, policies, and procedures are regularly reviewed as part of the overall IT governance review process.

The major challenge of implementing IT governance is that it might introduce cultural change in the enterprise. IT governance might result into implementation of new systems or processes which will require changes in the way employees carry out their daily activities. The enterprise will need to put in place programs to facilitate introduction of cultural change programs to encourage employees to accept change. Change is normally not easy to implement as there may be some influential people resisting change within the enterprise. Changes resulting from implementing technology might also mean introduction of new skills or some employees losing their jobs.

Auditing and Monitoring IT Governance

One of the key success factors of ensuring that IT governance is performing well is to regularly subject the process to an

IS audit. An IS audit will be able to uncover weaknesses in the implementation of IT governance and advise management on how to improve the IT governance process. Frequent audits add value to the enterprise and ensure that management is always compliant and improving governance processes.

The enterprise should ensure that the audit charter gives a clear mandate to the IS audit team on conducting IT governance audits. The audit charter should also give authority and timelines for the audits. Access to board information is critical to the audit. The IS audit team may find it difficult to make any meaningful audits if they have no access to information from the board on IT governance processes and outcomes. The IS auditors may be required to interview board members in order to validate their findings and make appropriate conclusions and recommendations.

Audit objectives for conducting IT governance audits should be clear so that the IS auditor understands what work is expected to be conducted. Often audit objectives are not clear, and IS auditors find themselves in conflict with the board and management. Use of kick-off meetings is important in order to ensure that there is a clear understanding and agreement on the engagement letter or audit objectives.

Audit objectives for an IT governance audit would include:

a) assessment of board involvement in resolving IT issues
b) review of IT performance reports by the board
c) involvement of the board in IT business planning
d) oversight role of the board in management of IT activities
e) assessment on the use of IT in the enterprise in order to achieve business goals.

The results of the IT governance audit should be communicated to all stakeholders unless there is a restriction from the board.

All stakeholders need to have a full understanding of the state of IT governance in the enterprise. This way, everyone will buy in and support implementation of IT governance and contribute to finding solutions and enhancing enterprise performance.

Clear IT performance metrics should be developed which will assist the IS auditor in assessing IT performance. The IS auditors should regularly review how these metrics are used and whether they effectively assist in analysing IT performance.

The board should put in place monitoring systems which will help in the monitoring of IT governance performance. Monitoring systems could be automated systems or manual methods. Monitoring can also be done through regular meetings which will review progress on IT governance activities.

IT Governance Standards

It was earlier indicated that consideration should be made as to which frameworks or standards should be used to implement IT governance in the enterprise. Enterprises might opt to use internally developed frameworks or use internationally accepted standards. In this chapter, we will focus on international standards.

ISO 38500 (IT governance standard) is a jointly published standard by the International Standards organisation (ISO) and International Electrotechnical Commission (IEC). The standard was published in 2003 and updated in 2004.

ISO 38500 can be used in all types and sizes of enterprises. The standard is also applicable in public and private enterprises. The standard is used to provide guidance to directors and executive management on the effective and efficient use of IT in the enterprises.

The ISO 38500 standard comprises definitions, principles, and a model. It sets out six principles for good corporate governance of IT which are responsibility, strategy, acquisition, performance, conformance, and human behaviour.

COBIT 5 is the latest release of the framework published by ISACA. The standard was published in 2013. COBIT is an integrated and comprehensive framework and does include some processes covered in ISO 38500 and ITIL. COBIT 5 covers the enterprise end to end, including all functions in an enterprise. All business functions are supported by the COBIT enablers.

ISACA has also published COBIT 5 for information security which builds on COBIT 5 framework. The new framework focuses on information security and provides a more detailed guidance for information security professionals and IS auditors.

The COBIT 5 framework can be used for the overall governance and management of IT in an enterprise. The framework consists of seven enablers and five processes. The enablers are used to enable information. Enablers are broadly defined as anything that can help to achieve the objectives of the enterprise.

The enablers include principles, policies, and frameworks; processes; organisational structures; culture, ethics, and behaviour; information; services, infrastructure, and applications; people, skills, and competencies.

The Information Technology Infrastructure Library (ITIL) is focused on IT service management. The current ITIL publication is known as ITIL 2011. The framework is published in a series of five core volumes which include ITIL service strategy, design, transition, operation, and improvement. ITIL processes are generic and not specific to any enterprise or industry. The framework is used to develop a baseline for planning, implementing, and measuring IT performance.

ITIL has a special focus on service-level management. Service-level management provides for continuous identifying, monitoring, and reviewing of the levels of IT services as specified in the service-level agreements (SLAs). Service-level management ensures that services are made available with both internal and external IT support.

The IS auditor can use the above standards to review implementation of IT governance. Each framework or standard has a particular focus and uses its own models to explain how IT governance should be implemented and operated.

Risk Management

In order to implement a good regime of IT governance, the board and management should have a good understanding and appreciation of the enterprise risk profile. An enterprise consists of various functions which work together to achieve set goals. Each function has its own risks which aggregate to overall enterprise risks.

The IS auditors also should have a good understanding of IT risk in order to perform an effective IS audit. By implementing and using IT in an enterprise, there are a number of IT risks the enterprise faces. In order to appreciate the risk exposure, the IS auditor may review existing risk management policies and the risk register. The IS auditor may also conduct a separate risk assessment in order to have a current understanding of the risk exposure and how IT risk is being managed in the enterprise.

There are a number of factors which the IS auditors may need to look at as they try to understand IT risk in the enterprise. Some of these factors may include (see figure 5.1):

a) availability of a risk policy in the enterprise
b) availability of an IT risk register
c) history of managing risks
d) type of business operations
e) current IT environment
f) planned IT environment
g) inherent IT risks
h) IT strategy
i) IT operations

Figure 5.1 Risk Factors

The risk appetite of the enterprise must be well understood and explained by both the board and management. Risk appetite might be a guide on how IT risk is being treated in the enterprise.

IT risks may include:

a) loss of data through accidental damage to computing equipment
b) loss of data through theft of storage devices
c) loss of data due to malfunctioning equipment
d) hackers having unauthorised access to IT systems in the enterprises
e) internal users deleting data with malicious intensions
f) failure of IT equipment
g) network failure
h) unavailability of critical IT staff

Figure 5.2 IT Risks

The IS auditor having understood the risk profile of the enterprise is in a position to conduct an effective audit of IT governance in relation to how IT risk is being managed in the enterprise. Due to the nature of technology, it is expected that new technologies will be introduced into the enterprise quite often and this implies that the risk exposure will change more regularly. This also means that the board and management should always be on the lookout for new risks due to the ever-changing technology.

Information Security

Information security is the securing of IT resources in the enterprise and protection of data and information. It is the responsibility of the board and senior management to ensure that information security governance is properly implemented in the enterprise using best practice. There are various standards which can be used to implement information security. We will discuss this topic in more detail in chapter 7.

Information security involves protection of different types of information such as soft copy, hard copy, voice, text, and video. Each type of information is protected using different strategies and tools. It is up to management to prioritize how they address security risks. Normally critical areas would receive higher priority and more resources in terms of protection.

In order to implement effective security measures, it is important to first understand IT risks existing in the enterprise. The outcome of an IT risk assessment would help determine how IT risks will be treated and what security measures to implement. Security measures should take into consideration the operations of the enterprise and changes to the internal or external environments. Risk assessments should be conducted more often in order to ensure that new risks are addressed in time.

It is the role of the board and management to ensure that enterprise resources are secured and data is protected. As part of its IT governance mandate, the board should ensure that everyone in the enterprise understands the importance of information security.

One of the tools for implementing information security in the enterprise is the security policy. Management should ensure that the information security policy is in place and supported by well-defined information security procedures. The benefits of implementing security are well known, but it is important to note that security is an enabler of business. Clients for example would be more interested in working with enterprises which protect their business transactions and personal information than enterprises which do not provide such comfort.

Limiting access to information to only authorised users is a key requirement for information security implementation. In most enterprises, access to data and information is through a user account and password. The IS auditor will find account and password policies which are used to implement access controls in most enterprises.

Personal privacy is important in that it protects customers' personal information from being used for other reasons than the reason the data was initially collected. Many countries have privacy laws which are used to make sure personal information is protected. Most enterprises have also developed privacy policies which are used to ensure that they are compliant with personal privacy laws.

Enterprises should also be protected from cybercrime, which is a common occurrence nowadays. Laws and various regulations related to cybercrime have been enacted in many countries, and international organisations such as the United Nations and European Union have been in the forefront of ensuring that countries enact cybercrime laws. The Internet has facilitated easy communication via email, websites, and social media, but despite this advantage, there are many security challenges which enterprises have to deal with as they make use of the Internet for business operations.

The role of the IS auditor would be to ensure that the board understands its mandate regarding information security. The board should regularly receive information on performance of security management. As part of IT governance audit, the IS auditor should review security in the enterprise and report to management or the board on findings and conclusions regularly.

CHAPTER 6

Auditing IT Risk Management

Overview

The IS auditor is required to have a good understanding of IT risk in the enterprise. The IS auditor is also regularly required to carry out IT risk audits because of the nature of IT risk. Many enterprises are dependent on IT to run and manage business operations, and it is for this reason that management requires assurance that IT systems are able to deliver required services and ensure that data and information is protected. IT should also add value to the enterprise in terms of growth, efficiency, and profitability.

Many enterprises have implemented IT risk frameworks in order to effectively manage IT risks beyond just implementing disaster recovery procedures. There are many ways of mitigating risks, which we shall review in this chapter. Our focus will be to cover key areas which should be considered when auditing IT risk.

The IS auditor should have a good understanding of the enterprise risk policy, the risk standards being used, and IT risk procedures which have been implemented. This information will enable the IS auditor to appreciate how IT risk is being managed in the enterprise.

This chapter will focus on what IS auditors should take into consideration when carrying out IT risk audits and enable management to have the required confidence in the IT systems which are used to automate business processes.

Objectives of Auditing IT Risk Management

It is important that we clearly outline some of the objectives of carrying out an IT risk audit. There are many reasons of course, but in this chapter, we will focus on a few key reasons. IT risk audit objectives may include:

1. to find out if an IT risk management framework exists and has been implemented in the enterprise
2. to determine that the IT risk management framework is included in the enterprise's overall risk management framework
3. determine which risk standards or best practices are used to implement risk management in the enterprise
4. establish that a risk register has been developed and covers all the functions in the enterprise
5. to find out whether the enterprise does regularly conduct risk assessments
6. to find out how identified risks are being mitigated and how residual risk is being treated by management
7. to investigate how risks and impact are being analysed in order to determine appropriate risk treatment
8. to determine how operational staff comply with various risk and operational procedures in order to ensure that risk is properly managed.

IT Risk Governance

The board and senior management should set the tone as to how risk will be managed in the enterprise and indicate what their risk appetite is in terms of what risks they can treat or accept as untreatable risk. The IS auditors will focus on a number of issues as they conduct an audit of IT risks which we will cover later in the chapter.

IT risk governance focuses on how the board and senior management handle IT risks in the enterprise. The IS auditor should first find out if the board does understand the risks the enterprise is facing. This can be done by interviewing board members and also reviewing records of board meetings. It is possible that views from the board members may differ for various reasons. But it is generally expected that the board and management will speak with one voice.

The board will set guidance through setting risk strategies, and management will operationalise the framework through implementation of policies and procedures. In order to ensure that risk strategies are being implemented as desired by the board, feedback should be given to the board through formal reports or briefings during board meetings. Senior management also should receive feedback from middle management on IT risk compliance.

It is the responsibility of both the board and management to monitor how IT risk management is being implemented in the enterprise. One way in which management would ensure that IT risk compliance is observed is by ensuring compliance with IT risk procedures. Management can put in place various mechanisms to ensure compliance.

In order to have effective monitoring of risks in the enterprise, management should ensure that regular IT risk audits are performed and reported to the board and senior management. It is recommended that independent IS auditors are used in addition to internal IS auditors. Independent IS auditors may discover issues which are not regularly reported by internal auditors or the risk management team when performing self-assessments.

Risk Management Committee

The board or senior management are normally busy people and do delegate the risk management responsibilities to a team of risk specialists and senior line managers or directors to handle the day-to-day management of risks. In some enterprises, the responsibility can be delegated to a committee with representation from various departments and supported by a risk management function headed by a director or manager.

The purpose of the risk management committee is to coordinate risk management activities in the enterprise, and they are also responsible for monitoring risks and ensure that new or changing risks are quickly identified and mitigated. The risk management committee will also give regular feedback to the board and senior management on risks in the enterprise.

It is recommended that representation on the risk management committee should be across the enterprise in order to ensure that all risk issues are picked up by the committee and reported to senior management and the board. The risk management function or department will conduct most of the routine work on behalf of the committee.

In smaller enterprises, the risk management function can be performed by other functions such as internal audit or a risk specialist contracted from outside the enterprise. The enterprise may also opt to employ a risk specialist to coordinate risk management activities on behalf of management.

The risk management committee should always be available to handle new risks or changes in risk exposure. This is why it is recommended that various departments should be represented on the risk management committee. Enterprises will always face different types of risks as they interact with clients, suppliers, regulators, and other enterprises. The IS auditor might look for evidence of availability of the committee members by checking who is on the committee, if they can be easily contacted by phone or email, and how often they interact with business operations to be able to identify and observe operations and how IT risk procedures are being implemented.

The IS auditor should hold interviews with the board, senior management, and the risk management committee in order to obtain an understanding of their appreciation of the enterprise's risk policy and procedures. A key consideration is how the board, senior management, and the risk management team monitor IT risk. It is possible that a risk management function could be available but without tools for monitoring risks. Enterprises are dynamic and face various problems which might cause new risks to arise.

The risk management committee should have a risk management program, which is implemented to deal with various risks. The program should include activities such as general IT risk assessments, IT project risk assessments, IT risk monitoring, IT risk profiling, change management, IT risk audits, and risk mitigation. The risk management function should consider developing a calendar of activities on how they shall conduct various risk activities.

The risk management committee should meet regularly to discuss business operations and review how risks are being managed. Ad hoc meetings with users can also be helpful as a way of monitoring risks. Front desk employees interact with clients and often come across information on what clients think of the enterprise and what the enterprise is doing and not doing.

The risk management committee will also be responsible for performing risk assessments. They are required to perform risk assessments at required times and when new IT projects are initiated or major changes are being made to existing systems.

We will discuss auditing IT risk assessments in more detail later in the chapter.

Change management controls are usually implemented when changes are being made to systems. The objective being that changes should be properly managed to enable rollback in the event that implementation goes wrong. The IS auditor would test if change management is being implemented by checking documentation on change controls, such as testing and approval of changes before they are deployed into production.

Implementing new projects or major changes or upgrades to existing systems mean that new risks might be introduced in the enterprise. A typical example would be that a new system which has been implemented may not have a system of alerting customers to pay their subscriptions. If the enterprise goes ahead to implement such a system, it might lose out on revenue as some clients may not pay in time or wait until their subscriptions expire. We will also discuss auditing IT projects in more detail later in the chapter.

Risk Management Frameworks

As we try to build up our understanding of auditing IT risk management, let us refer to common risk management standards which are used in enterprises to implement risk management. There are many standards which are used to implement risk management. In some enterprises, they implement their own internally developed standards, which are usually a mix of various international standards. A typical example is project risk. This standard can be found in different versions and being promoted by international organisations such as Project Management Institute through the PBOK framework, International Standards Organisation through ISO 31000, or Prince2 Foundation through Prince2.

The *ISO 31000* is one of the risk management standards which have been used to implement risk management in many enterprises. The standard is general purpose and can be used by any organisation and in any sector. The standard provides a process for managing risks and helps in the improvement of identifying risks, threats, and how to treat risk.

ISO/IEC 27005 is an information security standard which is deliberately risk-aligned in order to address many security risks. The standard provides guidelines for information security risk management and is based on ISO/IEC 27001, which is an information security management standard.

COBIT 5 for Risk has been developed to assist with the effective management of IT risk. The standard focuses on linking information technology risks with business performance. COBIT 5 for Risk defines IT risk as business risk, specifically, the business risk associated with the use, ownership, operation, involvement, influence, and adoption of IT within an enterprise.

ISO 22301 provide guidelines on the requirements for a management system to protect against the likelihood of disruptive incidents which might impact the enterprise. The standard is a business continuity management standard which prioritises threats to the enterprise.

IT Risk Assessment

IT risk assessment is the process of identifying risks in the IT environment. Enterprises do use various methods of carrying out risk assessments. One way of starting the process of risk assessment is by identifying critical and non-critical assets in the enterprise.

Critical assets are critical to the operation of the enterprise. In terms of IT assets, we can say that in an IT infrastructure, servers and databases running the ERP system are critical since they are used to support the business of the enterprise and also store data and information generated by the enterprise. Other critical assets would be the Internet if the business enterprise is dependent on the use of the Internet to conduct business. A distance-learning university usually would conduct all its business operations online. Students are able to register and work their way up to graduation by using an end-to-end e-learning system. In such a case, students in different countries can enrol and take courses online via the Internet. The Internet link and associated systems and devices, such as routers and firewalls, can be regarded as critical assets. Distance-learning universities cannot do without these assets and support students efficiently.

Another good example is Amazon.com which conducts its business on the Internet and cannot do without the Internet. The Amazon.com web portal can be said to be a critical asset as it is used as the interface with customers. Customers log in and purchase goods via the web portal. Maintaining a 24/7 Internet connection is also critical to the survival of the business.

Data and information in both examples given above are critical assets as their operations depend on the use of information and data generated by the enterprise. Without data and information, the two enterprises cannot communicate with its customers or conduct its business activities.

Non-critical assets are used in the enterprise to support core activities or can be said to be non-essential items. Printers can be said to be non-critical items in the distance-learning university example as the university can do without printers for some time compared to not having Internet traffic. Lack of Internet connectivity would mean no communication with students, and students would also not be able to access documents and their coursework. Other examples of non-critical assets in the distance-learning university would be office productivity software such as Microsoft Word or PowerPoint. Whilst these tools are essential in the office, they are not critical to the operation of the university compared to the student administration and course-delivery system.

Once critical assets have been identified, it is now possible to identify risks related to critical assets. It will not serve the enterprise any good to spend time trying to identify risks for non-critical assets because the enterprise can do without them for a while without major impact on the operations of the enterprise.

The risks to the university distance-learning systems include loss of data through damage to database systems, the web portal not being available because the system has been hacked, theft of data through internal collusion, and system malfunctioning.

Identified risks can be categorized as high, moderate, or low risk. High-risk assets require high-level attention whilst low-risk assets will require minimal attention, if not none, depending on its impact level. Categorizations of risk enables an enterprise to rate asset risks and determine how much effort should be applied in treating risks.

So far, we have identified critical assets and high-risk assets. Figure 6.1 below will help outline what we have achieved so far.

#	Asset	Criticality	Risk Rating	Cost
1	ERP System	Critical	High	High
2	Network Equipment	Critical	High	High
3	Data and Information	Critical	High	High
4	Office Application System	Non-Critical	Low	Low
5	Messaging System	Critical	High	High

6	Fire Suppression System	Critical	Low	Medium
7	Scanning Software	Non-Critical	Low	Low

Figure 6.1 List of Critical IT Assets

In the diagram above, assets 1, 2, 3, 5, and 6 are critical to the operations of the enterprise and have high replacement cost apart from the fire suppression system, which might have low to medium costs assuming the system is localised to the data centre. High-value assets are normally high-risk assets.

In order to assess the riskiness of a particular asset, the IS auditor should also identify threats to that asset. Some assets might have high risk but without possible threats. Where there are no threats, it would not be necessary to take particular measures to treat risks. It should be recognised that threats change over time and should be regularly monitored.

Threats take advantage of vulnerabilities in systems. Once threats have been identified, it is also important to know what vulnerabilities exist in the systems. Where there are no threats, it is possible that no action is required to fix vulnerabilities. It might not be worth the while and cost to try to fix vulnerabilities where there are no known threats.

The last part of risk assessment is to assess possible impact on assets in the event threats actually hit the enterprise and disable or destroy assets. High impact would mean devastation of company assets. Measures should be taken to ensure that operations are able to continue after impact either in a limited way or full service. Figure 6.2 shows the impact matrix and possible action to be taken by management.

#	Risk		Impact	Expected Action
1	High	Vs	Low	Minimum Action
2	High	Vs	Moderate	Action Required
3	High	Vs	High	Action Required
4	Low	Vs	Low	No Action
5	Low	Vs	Moderate	Action Required
6	Low	Vs	High	Action Required
7	Moderate	Vs	Low	No Action
8	Moderate	Vs	Moderate	Action Required
9	Moderate	Vs	High	Action Required

Figure 6.2 Impact Matrix

1. *High risk vs low impact* – Although the likelihood of the event happening is high, the impact on the enterprise is low. The enterprise might opt to accept the risk or take minimum or low-cost mitigation measures. An example would be backup data stored in a secure place. Whilst the risk is high that the data can be lost, the impact might be low because copies of the backups are kept in other sites.

2. *High risk vs moderate impact* – High risk combined with moderate impact requires action to be taken as the possibility of the event is there. A moderate impact might disable operations of the enterprise depending on criticality of the asset and its value. It is possible that an ERP system might have high risk because of the nature of the asset and the impact moderate if appropriate controls are applied.

3. *High risk vs high impact* – High risk assets include data and information. Loss of data can have a high impact as the enterprise would have to recreate the data, and this

might mean halting business operations for some time if the enterprise does not have an effective disaster recovery plan.

4. *Low risk vs low impact* – The enterprise might choose not to do anything and accept the risk if the risk is low and impact is low. The enterprise might be interested in assessing the impact on the enterprise even if the risk is low. There is a possibility that the risk might exist but with low impact that does not look bad. The enterprise might consider low-cost insurance to cover the low impact. An example would be loss of scanning software in the enterprise. The risk of losing a copy of the software is there but might be low and the impact is low in relation of operations of the company which might have the software already installed on the workstations.

5. *Low risk vs moderate impact* – A similar analysis and response might be taken in a low risk versus moderate impact situation. Since the impact is moderate and risk low, this means the impact is possible. Action should be taken to protect the asset. The enterprise can opt for low-cost mitigation since the risk is low. Having trained IT staff would be an example of low risk as we expect them to professionally manage an IT infrastructure.

6. *Low risks vs high impact* – Low risk means that the probability of an event is low and remotely possible. An example would be an earthquake happening in a non-earthquake zone, such as sub-Saharan Africa. The risk is low but impact is high. Designers of data centres or buildings may not worry very much about buildings being hit by earthquakes as the risk is low. Management would be worried about the high impact. Some action such as low-cost insurance can be taken just in case the

data centre was hit by an earthquake. It all depends on management if they can stomach the impact if it occurs.

7. *Moderate risk vs low impact* – In this scenario, the risk is moderate, which means that the chances of the event happening is possible. Management needs to take some action depending on the value and criticality of the asset. Risk can be reduced by applying measures such as access controls which limit access to authorised users only.

8. *Moderate risk vs moderate impact* – In this case, management would be more concerned with the moderate impact and its possible cost. Since the risk is moderate, the risk should be investigated further and management should put in place appropriate mitigation. An example would be loss of network equipment due to lightning. The risk might be reduced due to measures taken to protect the equipment, such as using surge protectors. The impact might also be reduced if spare equipment is kept for emergencies.

9. *Moderate risk vs high impact* – High impact automatically means that action should be taken to protect the asset. Moderate risk also means that chances are there that the event might take place. Secure email system might have moderate risk but high impact if the data is stolen or corrupted.

IT Risk Policy and Procedures

An enterprise should have a risk policy or framework so that they are able to implement an effective risk regime. The policy is a guide on how a risk framework will be implemented and managed in the enterprise. It is recommended that the policy should be based on accepted best practice or international standards such as ISO 31000, COBIT 5 for Risk, ISO 27005, and ISO 22301.

A policy is also a guide to the IS audit team so that they can have a clear understanding of management intention and risk appetite. The IS audit team might, in addition, appraise themselves on enterprise risk by reviewing IT risk processes implemented in the enterprise.

The IS auditor should not only read the risk policy but also verify that the policy is operational. There are various mechanisms which can indicate that the policy is operational, such as risk organisational structures, reports and reporting systems, and monitoring systems and procedures.

The format and contents of the risk strategy and policy will defer from one enterprise to the other but would generally contain the following details.

Risk strategy – The strategy will highlight how the board and management plan to manage risk in the enterprise. This will be expressed as part of the overall enterprise strategy. Risk strategy will also include risk governance.

Risk assessment – This is the identification of risks on enterprise assets and systems. Assets here include human assets who are trained and used by the enterprise as productive assets. Risk assessment can be carried out on a periodic basis or when new projects are being implemented.

Asset identification – Assets can be categorised as critical and non-critical assets. Management can also rate the risks of various assets.

Risk treatment – When risks are identified and impact assessed, it is possible to recommend an appropriate treatment. The policy will include various ways of treating risks or accepting risks.

Risk register – The register is basically a list of risks which the enterprise is facing based on the nature of its business and how these risks would be mitigated. The risk register would highlight various risks and related information.

Risk monitoring – The policy will also indicate how risks in the enterprise will be monitored, including procedures and tools which will be used. Risk monitoring would include regular IS audits by both internal and external auditors.

Risk plan – The policy will also indicate the need for a risk plan and how it will be implemented. Many large enterprises have fully functioning risk departments which develop and implement the risk plan.

The IS auditor will be required to review the implementation of a risk policy covering all or some of the areas as stipulated in the risk policy. The IS auditor will hold interviews with the board and senior management in order to determine how the policy is being implemented. Other stakeholders would include departmental heads, suppliers, and customers.

Enterprises implement and use risk procedures in order to establish controls in business processes. Where business procedures are properly implemented, it is likely that risk exposure will be minimized.

The IS auditor will, for example, be required to audit IT procedures, such as creation of user accounts. This procedure may require that a request for creation of a new user account is submitted by a user department for approval. The request is then authorised by the line manager and IT manager depending on the structure in the enterprise. The IT department will only create the new account upon completion of the authorisation procedures.

IT Project Risk

Enterprises implement various IT projects during a particular period, and each project comes with it various risks which have an impact on the overall risk profile of an enterprise. Failure of a project might have an impact on the operations of the enterprise.

Projects are initiated to update current systems in part or the whole system. In other cases, projects may be used to completely replace a system. In order to successfully implement projects, enterprises need to ensure that proper plans are developed for the projects.

We have seen private and public enterprises having massive project failures because of poor identification and treatment of risks. The overall risk policy of the enterprise should be a guide as to how risk will be managed in the enterprise. Projects might also have their own specific project risk goals which of course should not be in conflict with the enterprise risk policy.

Various project standards emphasises on the proper management of project risks throughout a project life span. Risks also change during the life of a project due to interaction with other projects, internal resources, and other stakeholders such as suppliers, consultants, external project team members, and government.

Planning is a key process when handling project risk as it takes into consideration various factors which might impact the project. One example is the availability of resources, such as human resources, financial resources, or equipment to be used on the project. Often project managers do not plan properly and encounter problems when the project is being implemented.

Project scope outlines what is to be accomplished on the project. Many projects fail because of poorly defined scope. Changes in scope whilst the project is being implemented need to be considered with risk management in mind. Changes to scope can possibly introduce new risks. The project manager should always be mindful of how scope is managed and factors which might lead to changes in scope.

The project manager should ensure that all changes in scope are subjected to a risk assessment before approval and implementation. The IS auditor's interest is to ensure that risk management procedures are properly implemented during a project so that risks do not negatively impact implementation of a project or operations of the enterprise.

Time management is a critical aspect of projects. If a project goes beyond the planned time for implementation, it is likely that project costs will also go up in terms of human resource costs and other operating costs.

Lack of adherence to quality is another aspect which might cause a project not to achieve its goals as indicated in the project plan. The IS auditor should also review implementation of quality assurance procedures on the project in order to ensure that quality is maintained.

Auditing project risk involves reviewing how the project was implemented and how risk for the projects was managed. Potential project risks are indentified during planning of the project and closely monitored during project implementation. It is possible that new risks might arise during implementation which might impact the project negatively or positively.

IT Risk Treatment

Once risks have been identified, the enterprise may now decide how to treat the identified risks. There are many ways of treating risks, and the board and senior management should guide the enterprise on their appetite for accepting risk.

When considering risk treatment, it is important to look at factors such as risk categorisation, threats, and vulnerabilities. These factors will help the enterprise determine what level of treatment to apply on a particular risk. Where threat levels are high, management might consider applying more complex measures in order to protect the enterprise. High risks are common where the enterprise is conducting its business on the Internet for example. Many hackers might be interested in bringing down the Internet site the enterprise is using or steal vital information from the enterprise databases.

One option the enterprise might consider is to avoid risks by, for example, ensuring that all IT equipment being purchased is through certified vendors. It is also an important consideration that IT staff are also trained to use and manage the equipment. Lack of trained staff might introduce risk in the enterprise as operation of equipment might not be up to the required standard.

The other way of treating risk is by transferring risk. Risk can be transferred through insurance, for example. If the enterprise has determined that there is risk of fire at the data centre, management might decide to insure the equipment and software used at the data centre. In the event of a disaster, the insurance company will pay for replacing the insured equipment and software. The enterprise can also transfer risk through equipment warranties. If there is a defect or system malfunction, the supplier can replace the equipment as per terms of the warranty.

IS auditors should ensure that the enterprise has put in place effective plans for ensuring risk transfer in order to protect the business. Risk transfers do not provide immediate relief as the replacement of equipment takes time unless there is an arrangement with suppliers of the systems.

The other measure management can use is by applying appropriate controls, such as implementing a disaster-recovery site. This will ensure that systems and data can be recovered in the shortest possible time in the event of an incident. Disaster-recovery sites might be expensive to set up but are worth the cost if the enterprise depends on IT systems for business operations.

An enterprise might decide to accept the risk if it is considered that it is less likely to occur and has low impact on the enterprise. A typical example is an earthquake happening in a zone where an earthquake has never happened in a hundred years. Management might take the position that the risk of damage to IT equipment is not likely because an earthquake might not happen. In the event that an earthquake does happen, the enterprise will accept damage to equipment and find money to replace the damaged equipment.

If the cost of treatment is higher than the assets the enterprise is trying to protect, management might also accept the risk and damage to equipment even if this means going out of business. A typical example would be replacing a brewery plant. Management might think that it is just too expensive to have a spare plant as a way of treating the risk and opt to accept the risk of the plant being rendered non-operational due to a disaster.

IT Risk Register

An enterprise will normally have a risk register which is used to record all risks identified in the enterprise. Each identified risk would include information such as risk rating, probability, threats, vulnerabilities, impact, risk treatment, and risk owners. Many professional organisations such as Project Management Institute and Prince2 Foundation provide recommendations as to what should be contained in the risk register. Enterprises are free to decide the content of their risk register depending on their risk exposure.

There are many software tools available which can be used for developing and maintaining risk registers. Use of software tools provides an easy way of managing and accessing risk information by all stakeholders. A risk register software tool can be deployed on the enterprise network platform for easy access by management, risk management team, internal auditors, and other external providers of assurance services. Using a risk register software, it is easy to monitor IT risk and various users and risk specialists on their risk activities, such as changes to IT systems or non-compliance to risk procedures.

A risk register will include a clear description of identified risks and linked to risk procedures. A link to risk procedures is helpful as it indicates what processes that particular risk is related to. It is possible that the enterprise might link business processes to various identified risk procedures and identified risks. A risk register should be updated often as activities take place in the enterprise. It is recommended that a risk function or specialist takes responsibility of updating the register as risks change every time due to interactions with the business environment.

The risk register should have a risk rating for each risk. The rating can be high, moderate, or low. Ratings will inform management or other users of this information on how to handle the risk. It is particularly important information when determining how to treat risk.

Criticality of IT assets is also one piece of important information when identifying and treating risks. Critical IT assets are high-value assets to the enterprise and are likely to have a high risk rating.

The probability of a risk occurring should be indentified and included on the risk register so that the enterprise can plan how to respond to such events. Where the risk is low, the enterprise can decide to accept the risk.

Potential threats also need to be identified and included on the risk register. Where there are risks but no threats, it is likely that the enterprise might choose to accept the risk. Potential threats normally take advantage of vulnerabilities which exist in the systems.

Possible impact is one attribute which should be included on the risk register. The impact on the enterprise is a critical event and requires monitoring regularly. It is also important to identify risk owners. These are people who are responsible for managing a particular risk.

A risk register is a useful tool for IS auditors as it provides the necessary information on the risks the enterprise is facing and how the enterprise is responding to the risks.

Example of IT Risk Register

Risk Category	Risk	Risk ID	Probability (1–5)	Impact (1–5)	Risk Rate (1–5)	Mitigation	Contingency	Action Time
Student Administration System	Loss of data	1A	4	5	5	Backup data	Use backed up data	< 5 minutes
Payment Receipting System	Wrong account posting	2A	2	1	1	Apply input control	Reverse transaction	< 48 hours
Transport Monitoring Software	Vehicle tracking failure	3A	2	5	2	Use secondary server	Use backup system	< 2 hours
Examination Processing System	Unauthorised posting of results	4A	4	5	3	Apply access controls	Reserve posting	< 24 hours
Email Server	Deleted emails	5A	2	5	4	Backup emails	Use backed up data	< 1 hour

Figure 6.3 IT Risk Register

IT Risk Management Plan

A risk management plan is a document which an enterprise develops in order to have an effective risk management response. The plan supports the enterprise's risk governance and strategy. The plan would also outline how the identified risks will be used to assess impact on the enterprise and the response from management.

The risk management plan is an important tool which should be available in hard copy or soft copy to all users in the enterprise. The plan may be integrated with a risk register so that links between risks and action plans can be clearly shown.

IT Risk Assessment Plan

A risk assessment plan is an annual plan which would include a risk assessment schedule outlining how often risk assessments should be conducted. One key requirement is the need to have risk assessments conducted every time new projects are being implemented as projects do have an impact on the enterprise. Such risk assessments would provide vital information on how the projects would impact the enterprise as a whole and if new projects introduced new risks in the enterprise.

Figure 6.4 shows four types of risk assessments. The first one is the annual risk assessment which can be conducted at the beginning of the year. The other risk is the periodic risk assessments which can be conducted every quarter and results compared with the annual risk assessment. Every project in the enterprise should be subjected to a risk assessment. Project risk assessments can be conducted at the beginning and at the end of the project. Project assessments can also be conducted more regularly depending on project requirements.

	Q1	Q2	Q3	Q4
Annual Risk Assessment	Y			
Periodic Risk Assessment	Y	Y	Y	Y
Project 1	Y			Y
Project 2	Y			Y

Figure 6.4 Risk Assessment Plan

Auditing a risk management plan and its implementation is essential as it will enable the IS auditor to assess how effective the plan is and how the enterprise is managing IT risk. The IS auditor may also be required to review the results of the annual and periodic assessments in addition to project-specific risk assessments.

CHAPTER 7

Auditing Information Security Management

Overview

Implementation of information security enables securing of IT assets and protection of data and information in the enterprise. In today's interconnected business environment, information is vital to the operation of enterprises as it is the oil which lubricates the enterprises.

IT governance enables effective use of IT in an enterprise, and information security is a component of IT governance. In order for an enterprise to implement information security effectively, it should be part of IT governance and the board and senior management should have a good understanding of how information security contributes to the success of the enterprise.

Information security risks are on the increase, and we are seeing more enterprises being hacked, including government and major enterprises in such countries as the USA and European countries. Frequently attacked systems are financial systems, such as online payment systems, credit card systems, and bank account records. Security risks are not only external to an enterprise but also internal risks do exist. An enterprise needs to have a security policy which will address both sources of threats.

Enterprises cannot operate effectively without securing its resources and those of its customers. It is widely accepted by security professionals that security is an enabler of business and should be used as such. Security will not operate in a vacuum but also involves employees and various supporting systems which make the enterprise work.

An IS auditor plays an important role by ensuring that information security is properly implemented in the enterprise and that it does provide security to business operation and protection of data and information. Enterprises do use IS auditors to audit information security at planned intervals and when there is a requirement for such an audit. Enterprises use various security procedures in order to implement security, and IS auditors are required to audit these procedures to determine the effectiveness of security in the enterprise. We will assess these security procedures and highlight what type of evidence is required to be collected to support the IS auditor's findings, conclusions, and recommendations.

The IS auditor would normally start the audit by focusing on security risks in the enterprise and should have a good appreciation of security risks in the enterprise. The IS auditor would do this by reviewing documentation on security risks and interviewing information security management or other members of senior management. An important document which the IS auditor should read is a recent IT risk assessment report. Such a report would give an indication of the current risk position of the enterprise and also link the assessment to an existing risk profile. The recent risk assessment can be used to update the existing risk profile.

In this chapter, we will look at areas the IS auditor is required to review in order to conduct an effective information security audit. The objectives of auditing information security are many, and we will refer to them throughout the chapter so that you can appreciate the importance of implementing security in the enterprise.

Information Security Policy

The first action an IS auditor would take is to review the information security strategy the enterprise has in place. This information can be found in the IT strategy document or by discussing with senior management. It would also be ideal for the IS auditor to review other documentation, such as board and management minutes, which might shed some light on how information security strategies have been dealt with over the previous periods at board and senior-management level.

The board and senior management would generally give a good indication as to how they are approaching security in the enterprise and their commitment to securing enterprise resources.

To support the enterprise information security strategy, senior management would put in place an information security policy. The policy is used to guide and implement information security in the enterprise. This is a guide to all functions and users in order to ensure that security is effectively implemented.

The information security strategy and policy should show a clear link between the two documents, and there should be no conflict between the two documents. The policy should reflect the spirit of the strategy. One would say that the strategy is the guide for developing a policy. The IS auditor should review the two documents and ensure that their objectives are not in conflict. If the two documents are in conflict, the IS auditor should raise the issue with management.

The second important review the IS auditor would undertake before performing any further detailed security audit is to confirm existence and implementation of the policy. Senior management would provide this confirmation through signed documents or minutes of the board or management meeting. It is recommended that the IS auditor holds discussions with board members or senior management so that they might provide some insight into the development and implementation of the security policy. Reading a policy document might not provide background information which the IS auditor would get by interviewing key people involved in implementing security in the enterprise.

The IS auditor should also check that the policy is reviewed at regular intervals or according to enterprise policy on review of policies. The policy should always be current and reflect changes in the enterprise. If the enterprise undergoes a major change in business processes and IT systems, this might impact the security policy of the enterprise.

The IS auditor should also check that the security policy has been properly implemented and documented. In many enterprises, IS auditors would find that a policy does exist but not implemented. The IS auditor would also come across situations where only parts of the policy have been implemented. It is important that the IS auditor has a good understanding of the level of implementation of security policy. This information can be collected from the security function and validated by management and employees from various functions in the enterprise. It should be noted that information security is about everyone in the enterprise that is, from the board to the lowest employee.

It is recommended that the security policy developed and implemented by the enterprise should be based on accepted best practice or international standard. There are various security standards which can be used, and common ones include ISO/IEC 27001, ISO/IEC 27014, ISO/IEC 17799, and BS 7799. Other information technology management international frameworks such as COBIT and ITIL have information security incorporated in the frameworks. ISACA has developed COBIT 5 for information security, which focuses on the management of information security in the enterprise and to support business processes. The 27000 series standards include various areas of security and can be found on the ISO international standards website. Below is the structure of ISO 27001:2013 standard. Enterprises have the option of implementing all or part of the standard as required by management.

Structure of ISO 27001:2013 standard

Figure 7.1 Structure of ISO 27001:2013

Auditing a security policy is one important activity of ensuring that an information security infrastructure is effective in securing business resources and protecting data and information. Most enterprises implement security policies which are generally in line with ISO security standards such as ISO 27001. The IS auditor will find that other enterprises make modifications to the standards to fit their unique operations. Senior management will regularly request IS auditors to review the implementation or performance of the policy or some parts of the policy. Senior management, being custodian of the security policy, will determine the audit objectives and expected outcomes.

With reference to the chart above, let us review what the IS auditor is required to do as regards the components of the ISO 27001:2013 standard.

- *Information Security Policies* – A policy is a guide developed by management on how security should be implemented and managed in the enterprise. The IS auditor will be required to have a good understanding of the policy and be able to effectively audit the policy and its implementation.

- *Organisation of Information Security* – The enterprise should have an information security structure which can be used to implement and manage security in the enterprise. Without a security structure, information security might not be implemented effectively. The organisation could be a full-fledged department headed by a director or manager. In smaller enterprises, the security function can be managed by a security coordinator in a full- or part-time role. The IS auditor should review the control structure of the security organisation and also regularly assess its effectiveness in managing security in the enterprise.

- *Human Resource Security* – Procedures need to be put in place which will ensure that correct and qualified human resources are recruited by the enterprise. The procedures will also ensure that the human resources comply with various security policies. The IS auditor is required to ensure that security procedures are in place for recruitment of staff, and security is one of the considerations when hiring employees.

- *Asset Management* – IT assets need to be protected, and the IS auditor should ensure that procedures are available for protecting IT assets. IT assets are critical to the operation of the enterprise. Maintenance of an IT asset register is one way of ensuring that IT assets are tracked and monitored.

- *Access Controls* – Access controls ensure that only authorised users have access to data and information. The IS auditor should regularly review access rights in order to ensure that authorised users have appropriate access to the systems. The IS auditor should also ensure that all users are authorised by management.

- *Cryptography* – The enterprise should ensure that cryptographic controls are implemented and effectively managed in order to protect systems and data during transmission from internal and external threats. The role of the IS auditor would be to assess the implementation and effectiveness of cryptographic controls. The IS auditor should ensure that the enterprise has a cryptography control policy in place which can be used to implement and manage systems which require the use of cryptography.

- *Physical and Environmental Security* – The enterprise should ensure that appropriate physical and environmental security controls are in place, which include protection of data centres and disaster recovery sites. The IS auditor should regularly review physical and environmental controls in order to ensure protection of data centres, recovery sites and other critical IT rooms.

- *Operations Security* – The enterprise should ensure that business and IT operations are secure by implementing appropriate security measures. Security should include network security, data backup, systems monitoring, and security of computing equipment used to process data and facilitate communication. The IS auditor's role includes reviewing implementation of security operations in the enterprise. The IS auditor should ensure that appropriate security is provided to IT operations, such as physical and logical access controls. The IS auditor would also be required to review operational procedures and responsibilities.

- *Communications Security* – The enterprise should ensure that communications between networks are secure. Communication between enterprises is conducted using several methods such as email, text, conversations, document sharing, voice, and video. The IS auditor has a role of reviewing security of communication systems so that data and information is protected.

- *Information Systems Acquisition, Development, and Maintenance* – The IS auditor should get involved in the deployment of systems from procurement up to maintenance and ensure that appropriate controls are implemented. System deployment includes a number of activities which require review by the IS auditor in order to ensure appropriate security controls are included and effective.

- *Supplier Relationships* – Enterprises should ensure that supplier relationships are protected by having service-level agreements, which will ensure that agreed services are provided by suppliers in a secure and protected environment. Nowadays enterprises rely on third parties to provide information technology services. It is the responsibility of the IS auditor to regularly review supplier relationships in order to ensure provision of secure and appropriate services.

- *Information Security Incident* – Incident management is critical to the management of security. The enterprise should be able to have a robust record of incidents if they have a system for recording and resolving incidents. Many enterprises today use electronic systems to manage incidents. The IS auditor is required to review the incident management systems to assess their effectiveness in the enterprise.

- *Business Continuity Management* – An enterprise should put in place a business continuity management plan which will ensure that the business continues operations in the event of a disaster. Business continuity involves the whole enterprise and includes recovery of IT systems which is normally included under disaster recovery. The IS auditor using appropriate tools is required to review implementation and management of the enterprise business continuity plan.

- *Compliance* – The enterprise should ensure compliance with the IT policy and procedures developed and implemented by the enterprise. It also involves compliance with regulation and laws of the country. Most countries have enacted laws concerning personal privacy, keeping of electronic records, and protection of information. It is the role of the IS auditor to ensure that the enterprise is in compliance with policies, regulations, and laws through regular audits.

Security Management Structure

In order to have an effective implementation of security in the enterprise, it is recommended that a suitable organisational structure is put in place to support operations of information security. The IS auditor should review the security organisation in order to determine that it is suitable for implementing and maintaining a good security infrastructure.

The overall responsibility of ensuring security in the enterprise rests with the board of directors who will issue directives through senior management. The structure of the security function will depend on the size of the enterprise and level of security required in the enterprise. Very large enterprises such as multinational corporations usually have formal functions with several full-time employees. Medium to small enterprises might have one or two security specialists. In other small enterprises, the security function might use part-time employees to manage security who themselves might have other full-time functions in the enterprise. It is also common to see consultants from outside the enterprise being used as security specialist. Figure 7.2 shows a possible structure in a large enterprise with a full-time security department headed by a director or manager.

The board which has overall responsibility for security might opt to appoint a committee of the board to be in charge of security matters in the enterprise. The committee might comprise of members of the board and some senior management officials. The security committee should have clear terms of reference and mandate from the board. In order to ensure that the committee has control of the security function, all reports and feedback to the board should be through the security committee. Different reporting lines would create parallel structures and cause conflicts in the management of security in the enterprise.

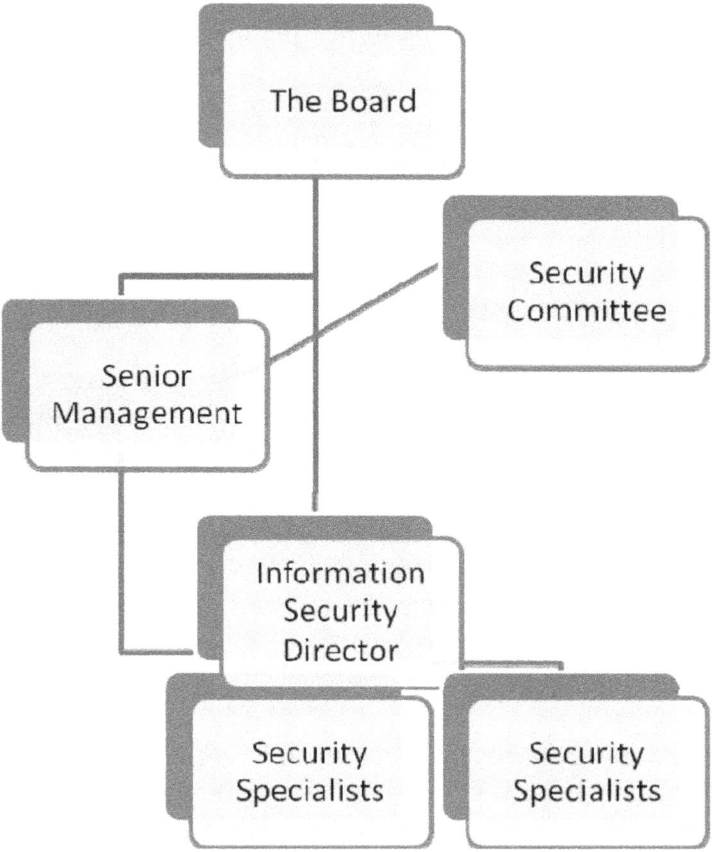

Figure 7.2 Information Security Organisation

The IS auditor should take particular interest in how the board and security committee conduct its business of ensuring security for the enterprise. The IS auditor should arrange interviews with members of the board or security committee so that he can have a good understanding of the intentions of the board regarding security. The IS auditor can also conduct some fact-finding by reviewing previous board and committee documentation.

The IS auditor should also review the terms of reference of the security committee. The committee might be handicapped if it does not have full authority to act or make decisions on behalf of the board. Security can be a fluid activity, and decisions in many cases need to be made in a timely manner in order to protect and secure enterprise resources. The committee should also be in a position to receive timely information which it can use to make decisions.

The security committee is in between the board and the management. Senior management reports to the board on all matters of the business and also has representation on the security committee which is a subcommittee of the board. In some enterprises, senior management might have its own security team within the senior management team. This is largely applicable in large enterprises where senior management has more involvement in security matters. In another scenario, senior management might have members sitting on the security committee instead of the having a security team at senior-management level.

The audit of senior management's security responsibilities should be the same as outlined at board and security-committee level. The level of detail will definitely be higher considering that the role of senior management is more operational than that of the board and security committee. The IS auditor should also review how regular senior management receives security reports from the security committee and security department. This ordinarily would be the same report unless there are specific requirements to submit different reports to the security committee and senior management.

The IS auditor should also take particular interest in the content of the security reports so that the security function provides senior management and the security committee with sufficient information to make decisions at that level. It is common to find that senior management receive too much or little information. The frequency of reporting should also be a subject of audit as it will indicate how often senior management receives reports.

It is also important to assess whether there is feedback from senior management on the various reports which they receive from the security function. The effectiveness of the security function will depend on how information received by senior management is used to ensure security of the enterprise.

In most large enterprises, the IS auditor will find a full-time security function or department which handles everyday implementation, management, and monitoring of security in the enterprise. The department is responsible for generating most of the security reports and also is involved in management of security in the enterprise. The function will also monitor all security activities and make necessary recommendations to management.

Within the security department, there are various security specialists who work on specific security tasks, such as implementation, operations, reviewing, monitoring, compliance, and reporting. In smaller enterprises, these responsibilities can be performed by a single security specialist or a part-time security coordinator. External security coordinators are often hired by enterprises to perform similar functions as internal security specialists.

Auditors reviewing work of a security function would have to conduct detailed investigations as the department generates a lot of security data and is involved in managing various areas of security. What is important here is that the IS auditor should be able to collect all necessary evidence to support assertions made by security management. There are various security areas the IS auditor might review, and this can be done over a specific period and focusing on different areas at a time.

Information Security Awareness Program

Information security involves all users in the enterprise, and they should be made aware of their responsibilities as regards security. Information security, when it involves all stakeholders, is more robust. It is often said that the weakest security point in an enterprise is the user or the employee. Most often efforts to secure the enterprise are more focused on external threats than internal threats. We have seen from security incident statistics that internal threats are also on the increase especially where there is collusion between external parties and employees. Employees either motivated by financial gain or just out of ignorance have given out passwords and other internal security information to outsiders who later hack into enterprise systems.

Enterprises have seen emergence of new threats due to the use of new technologies, such as wearable technologies. These technologies could be cameras, sensors, health monitors or smartwatches which employees wear in the office. Some of these technologies use Bluetooth for communication, which is also used by other office equipment. It is possible that security can be compromised by vulnerabilities existing in the software, configurations of these wearable technologies or from unprotected devices which might connect to rogue Bluetooth devices.

The purpose of security awareness is to provide education to users on security measures the enterprise has put in place. In addition, it is important that security training is also provided to IT professionals responsible for implementing security technologies.

The content of security training to be provided to all users in the enterprise (that includes the board and senior management) should be based on the approved information security policy and procedures used in the enterprise. Users should be aware of the security requirements which management has put in place. It is also essential that users are taken through all possible practical examples of maintaining security in the enterprise. The content of security training should be updated whenever new information is available, which would assist in securing information assets. New viruses are detected every day, and it is the responsibility of the information security team that this information is made available to the users as soon as it is available.

Some important aspects about security training include how training is delivered to users especially busy people like those in senior management. It is recommended that training providers use different methods of training to ensure that the message is effectively delivered. For example trainers can make use of workshop-style delivery to new joiners and email communication to existing employees or make use of social media, such as Facebook, Twitter, and YouTube. Some enterprises have made use of newsletters or other forms of newsflash to communicate with users. Each enterprise has different ways of effectively delivering training. It is the role of the IS auditor to assess how effective this training is by interviewing users and managers responsible for such training programs. The IS auditor can use various techniques to assess effectiveness of security awareness training.

The frequency of awareness training programs depends on the type of training and content. Where training is delivered in short sessions and focusing on different topics, it is possible that training can be frequent. Some enterprises do make use of video presentations which users download from the internal portals or enrol for training online.

Information Security Procedures

There are various security procedures an enterprise can use to ensure that security is achieved in the enterprise. In this section, we will review selected procedures so that we can highlight the approach an IS auditor could take and what evidence can be obtain to support assertions made by management.

Access Controls

IS auditors, whenever they are auditing security controls, will come across the requirement to audit access controls. Access controls are used to ensure that only authorised users have access to IT systems, data, and information. The assessment of access controls involve reviewing granting and revoking of user access, allocation of user rights, password policy, and account policy.

The enterprise is required to have a policy on access controls at network and application system levels. Most enterprises have dual access controls which are applied at network operating system level and at application system level. Where enterprises do not use an integrated system, such as an ERP system, access controls will have to be implemented in each application system used in the enterprise. IS auditors, when reviewing access controls, will be required to collect evidence from network operating systems and application systems. This information can be collected from documentation prepared by the IT function or by extracting data from the security domain controller. Access control information can also be extracted from application systems and exported to other application systems such as Word, PDF, or Excel.

The IS auditor should also review application systems audit trails so that any violation of access controls can be identified and analysed. Audit logs can have huge volumes of data collected every day, and it is recommended that audit tools are used for such exercises in order to perform an effective and efficient analysis of data and in a timely manner.

Backups

In order to ensure that enterprise data and information is protected, the IT function is required to perform backups according to backup policy. In highly automated enterprises and where recovery time is very short, backups are done frequently or every few seconds by making use of snapshots to make differential backups.

It is recommended that the IS auditor begins the audit of backups with the review of the backup policy and assess whether it is being implemented according to the expectations of management. Auditors audit backup policy and procedures in order to ensure that backups are being performed as per policy and that the enterprise is able to recover in the event of an incident impacting on data, information, or IT facilities. Backup operations generate information which IS auditors can use as evidence, such as daily backup records (manual or electronic), testing of backups, storage of backups, and monitoring of backup operations.

Network Security

Network security involves securing IT assets and data on the enterprise computer network. There are various threats which can harm the enterprise in terms of its resources, such as data and information. Typical threats from outside the enterprise network are hackers who are interested in stealing data or destroying hardware and software used by the enterprise to conduct its business.

Firewalls are security devices which are used to prevent unauthorised outsiders from accessing internal network resources of an enterprise. There are various types of firewalls which can be installed to handle this task. There are mainly two types of firewalls, which are hardware firewalls and software firewalls, although in real terms, all firewalls use software which either run on a dedicated hardware device or on a server.

In order to ensure effective management of network security, firewalls should be monitored. Monitoring will provide information to management on how effective the devices are in protecting the enterprise. Without monitoring, the enterprise will not know whether the devices are effectively protecting the enterprise. The enterprise can use software tools which can extract data from firewalls and display it in readable form such as figures and graphs. The security department can regularly summarise and comment on the data and provide advice to management.

Network security can also be used to ensure that data is properly routed within the internal network by using devices such as network switches and routers. These devices can be configured in such a way that traffic between computer devices is routed according to secure and defined routes.

As part of its security strategy, the enterprise may install intrusion detection and prevention systems which will ensure that intruders are detected or prevented from accessing network resources.

The IS auditor will have access to data generated by various devices which he can use as evidence to support compliance with security policies and procedures. The data can also be used to verify that security systems are working as planned.

Application System Security

Security controls can also be applied specifically to application systems besides network-level security controls. One of the common security controls are access controls. These are applied on the basis of need to know. Only authorised users are given access to use application systems.

Security hardening is a feature which can be used to ensure that the application systems and databases are secure and robust. This can be done by applying patches to the application systems, which are normally developed by software vendors or other third-party service providers. Closing unused ports on the application server can also be a useful way of enhancing application security.

Security controls can be embedded in business processes to ensure that business activities are carried out in a controlled and secure manner. An example would be how customers make payment for services they would like to access. The enterprise offering services to its customers would provide a secure platform on which payments can be made and funds deposited in designated accounts at the bank. The IS auditor would use an application controls audit to review various applications in addition to specific application security audits.

Patch Management

Patch management is a process of implementing security and system updates after the main application system has been implemented. There are various vulnerabilities which are discovered after software has been released. This applies to both operating and application systems.

It is important that patching of software is carried out in a controlled environment which includes testing of patches in a test environment before they are deployed on production systems. Patches should be tested so that the enterprise is certain and confident that the patches will not introduce other problems. It is common to find users and some IT professionals taking it for granted that patches published by software developers or vendors will not cause problems. Usually problems arise from using different technologies and software platforms which might cause conflicts after a patch is applied.

In order to reduce costs, some enterprises use virtual servers as test environments which are essentially using the same hardware and same operating systems running virtual software. There are various types of virtual software on the market which can be used to build virtual test environments.

Once patches have been tested, they can be deployed using distribution software which will push the patches to all workstations and servers. It is easy to apply the patches using distribution software as all computers will receive the patches at the same time. Common patch management software includes System Centre Configuration Manager (SCCM or ConfigMgr) and Systems Management Server (SMS) produced by Microsoft. There are also many other commercial software which are used for deploying patches.

Patching servers and workstations is much easier if the enterprise is using the same type of client and server operating system throughout the enterprise. Due to new technologies coming on the market which are deployed in our work environments, such as smartphones and wearable devices, the IS auditor will find different operating systems which will require a different strategy and approach regarding patching.

Patching is not only for operating systems, but it can also be deployed to patch application software such as ERP systems or other applications used in the enterprise. A strategy needs to be developed for patching application systems. It is more challenging for enterprises running many and different application systems as each will need a different way of applying the patches.

IS auditors would be keen to know that patches are tested before being deployed. Evidence can be obtained from patch management documentation. It is recommended that the IT function should maintain a record of patches which have been tested and deployed so that IS auditors can review the records in addition to checking deployed patches on the actual operating or application systems. The records would include date patches were tested, approval of testing, and type of tests. The IS auditor should also ensure that the enterprise has clear procedures on how to identify required patches, testing of patches, and finally deploying of patches.

Antivirus Management

Enterprises should ensure that the IT environment is protected from viruses and other similar programs. Viruses do infect computers and render them unusable in many cases. If the IT environment is not managed properly, it can easily be brought down by viruses which can also spread to other enterprises through sharing of files and email.

There are new viruses being discovered every day, and many of them are very dangerous viruses which can be devastating to an IT environment. Companies which produce antivirus solutions are always on the lookout for new viruses, and they do quickly produce new definitions and make them available so that enterprises can protect their IT systems against new viruses.

There are various types of viruses, and each needs a different strategy of eradication. Some of the many variants of viruses include:

#	Virus Type	Description
1	Worms	Worms spread from one computer to the other unaided using the computer transport system. The worm has the capability to replicate itself and infect many files on computers and external storage devices.
2	Malware	Malware (**mal**icious soft**ware**) steal information on infected computers such as login and credit card information. Malware includes such variants as spyware and adware.
3	Key Loggers	Key loggers record (or log) keystrokes on a keyboard connected to an infected computer without the users knowing in order to steal passwords or credit card information.
4	Trojans	A Trojan appears to be a legitimate file or software but behaves in a different way when installed or copied on a computer, such as deleting, blocking, or corrupting files.
5	Viruses	A computer virus attaches itself to a program file or document allowing it to spread as the files are copied across computers.
6	Time Bomb	A time bomb virus executes a malicious function at a specified time and date. The malicious function may include deleting files or corrupting files.

7	Denial of Service (DOS) attack	The DOS attack is carried out on an infected computer or network by flooding it with several requests which blocks the computer from operating normally.
8	Backdoor	A backdoor virus enters a computer without being detected and opens ports which are used by third parties to control or steal information.
9	Spam	Email spam is the sending of identical mail messages to different recipients from infected computers or user email accounts. Spam email can also contain links which can lead to phishing websites hosting malware.
10	Adware	Adware pops up unwanted advertisements on infected computers.

Figure 7.3 Types of Viruses

In order to properly manage and control virus infections, an enterprise needs to invest in a good and robust antivirus software. There are many antivirus solutions on the market ranging from single-user software to large enterprise solutions which can be used to manage thousands of users. An enterprise needs to investigate antivirus solutions on the market and select an appropriate solution.

Antivirus software includes virus definition files which require to be updated often. Most antivirus software can be configured to update virus definitions as soon as they are made available by antivirus solution developers. The solutions can also be configured to update on a timely basis such as daily or weekly.

Enterprises have the option of deploying managed and unmanaged antivirus solutions. Managed systems are centrally controlled, and most configurations are done on the server. Unmanaged solutions are configured on the workstation and are not centrally managed. The enterprise might also configure the antivirus application to auto scan at specified intervals, such as daily or every hour. Antivirus software can be set to automatically scan all storage devices connected to the computer, such as memory sticks or external storage.

Enterprises should develop enterprise antivirus management policies in order to effectively address issues of viruses in enterprises. Antivirus procedures are also required in order to ensure that users adhere to specific ways of dealing with viruses. Large enterprises employ full-time antivirus specialists, who are responsible for day-to-day management of antivirus security. Their responsibilities include ensuring that users are aware of how to handle virus incidents, sending user alerts, repairing virus-infected computers, and preparing reports on virus infections and management.

User training is an effective way of managing viruses in an enterprise. An enterprise should ensure that users are aware of virus incidents and how to respond. The enterprise, through established procedures, should make sure that there are clear escalation procedures in the event of infections. In most enterprises, antivirus protection is part of security awareness training for new and old users.

The IS auditor should collect evidence on how the enterprise is managing the antivirus security environment. Statistics on virus infections can be obtained from the antivirus application system which automatically collects and reports on various virus incidents. The IS auditor can also review reports prepared by the IT function and antivirus security specialists as part of the audit. Interviewing users is also a good source of information. It is always recommended that IS auditors randomly check user computers to test the effectiveness of the antivirus management practices in the enterprise.

Internet Security

Internet security relates to the securing of Internet systems such as websites, web browsers, email, and other business tools used by an enterprise which rely on the Internet. Most enterprises today are highly dependent on the use of the Internet to conduct business. The Internet has also brought many risks as well as benefits. Often we hear of enterprises being hacked by known or unknown persons or organisations. Many enterprises have lost millions of dollars through Internet fraud. Individual customers also have been hit by Internet fraudsters who skim credit card information and later use the information to steal money or make payments for services.

Enterprises need to set up robust cybersecurity procedures in order to ensure that company resources and customers are protected. Use of firewalls, intrusion detection and prevention systems, and Internet security applications are useful in order to ensure that enhanced security is available in the enterprise.

Regular monitoring of various security appliances is recommended as it enables the enterprise to have required statistics on threats the company is facing and also enable the enterprises to take appropriate action to protect the resources which are used by the enterprise.

The IS auditor is required to audit how users in the enterprise use the Internet and how the enterprise protects its resources from threats from the Internet. There are various types of information which the IS auditor can use in order to verify how the enterprise is complying with Internet security procedures.

Many users access the Internet on a daily basis from their offices, homes, and phones. They need to be made aware of the dangers of the Internet and how to protect their computers. Regular security alerts are always important in order to warn users on news breakouts on viruses or hacking incidents. Enlightened users help in the fight for a secure and protected environment.

Personal Privacy and Data Protection

Personal privacy is about protecting customer data collected by virtue of business transactions. Various countries have enacted laws which protect information collected from customers. Enterprises also have developed personal privacy policies and procedures which are used to ensure that enterprises comply with national laws.

Personal privacy laws restrict use of information obtained from customers to only authorised use. For example if the information was collected for health reasons, that information shall not be used for any other reason unless permitted by the owner. In some countries, personal privacy laws are so complex that full-time specialists are employed to handle personal privacy issues.

Over time the enterprise will collect information on how personal privacy is implemented in the enterprise, and IS auditors are required to assess this information. In some enterprises, IS auditors are required to review personal privacy activities annually or half yearly for enterprises which hold sensitive personal information.

Database Security

Databases are used to store data and information which is generated by the enterprise by virtue of conducting business operations. Databases are normally attached to application systems, such as ERP systems, which are used to capture and process data.

There are various types of databases ranging from small flat file databases to large relational databases which can store large volumes of data. Enterprises, especially multinational corporations, generate billions of bytes of data each day, and this data needs to be kept in a structured way using database systems. Because of the important role databases play, enterprises take particular care to secure databases.

Databases store different types of data and information. The first data type is standing data which define fields and other pieces of data which are of a permanent nature. The other form of data is raw business data which is captured into the system but not processed. There is also processed data sitting on the database which we often refer to as information.

It is the obligation of the enterprise to ensure that the databases are secure and information is protected. There are various measures which are taken to secure databases, such as closing ports which are not in use, applying security controls, and ensuring security procedures around the databases are complied with.

The role of the IS auditor is to ensure that the databases are secure and the information on the database is protected. IS auditors often perform specialised database audits which require specialised skills. Evidence on database security can be obtained from the database logs and by reviewing how the databases were configured. The enterprise would, before installing the database, establish a security baseline which can be used to measure actual performance against planned performance. This information can be used to assess performance of the databases in relation to security requirements.

Operating System Security

Operating systems are used to manage and control computer systems. Operating systems perform vital operations of managing computing devices. Today many other devices use operating systems such as smartphones, smartwatches, electronic gadgets, motor vehicle control systems, and health-monitoring devices. Operating systems also provide security to data and other systems used on the computer, such as application software.

Operating systems have many features which make our computers perform many functions, such as managing application software, enabling network connections, multitasking, printing, saving files, and handling input and output of information.

There are many types of operating systems starting from those which are used to manage small systems, such as smartwatches, to large and complex systems, such as onboard computers on a Boeing 777 or Airbus 380 aircraft. Computers used in an office have operating systems for workstations, such as laptops, tablets, or personal computers. There are also network operating systems which are used to manage office networks which connect wide area networks across geographical boundaries or across continents. A typical example would be a company like Microsoft which has offices on all continents.

Operating systems are secured by applying various security measures such as hardening the operating systems which involves closing unused ports, disabling unused functions, installing antivirus software, intrusion detection tools and patching the systems with recommended patches from software developers.

The IS auditor can use information generated by various tools and logs on the operating systems to perform an audit of operating systems. Client operating systems produce a lot of valuable information which the IS auditor can make use of not only for auditing client operating systems but also application systems and network operating systems.

Security Monitoring

In order to ensure effective IT security in the enterprise, a security monitoring policy needs to be developed which can be used to monitor how security is being managed. Regular monitoring of security provides assurance that management has oversight over security management in the enterprise. It should be noted that security risks are ever-changing and an enterprise will always face new risks as they conduct business operations. Enterprises can also make use of security self-assessments in order to ensure compliance with security policies and procedures.

In addition to implementing security measures, enterprises can also rely on IS auditing services to provide assurance to management. Enterprises can make use of the internal IS audit function to conduct regular review of security. In addition, enterprises can make use of external IS auditors or security specialists to complement the work of internal IS auditors.

CHAPTER 8

Auditor Involvement in Systems Deployment

Overview

Enterprises throughout their life cycle implement various IT projects designed to automate and improve performance of the enterprise. These could be new projects or projects designed to upgrade existing systems. Quite often systems are upgraded in order to incorporate new business processes, additional controls, or new technologies.

Often IS auditors are not involved in development or deployment of systems and are only called upon when systems are either ready for deployment or already in operation. With the advancement of technology and dependence on IT systems (which are the lifeline of enterprises today), it is important that IS auditors are involved in system deployment in order to ensure that IT controls, security, and other important system features are included in the new or upgraded systems. The role of the IS auditor is not to get involved in the design and implementation of the systems but to ensure that the required controls, security, and user specifications are incorporated in the systems being deployed and that the systems are properly tested.

Standards and guidelines have been developed to guide IS auditor involvement in systems deployment by ISACA and other professional associations. It is important that IS auditors use standards and guidelines as they provide details of the requirements for auditing systems deployment. Often you will find IS auditors doing more than they are required to do on IT projects.

In order to have a clear understanding of the auditors' involvement in systems deployment, we shall use the systems development life cycle (SDLC) activities. You will note that there are a standard number of activities you would find in a traditional life cycle. Below is an extended SDLC, which we will use to explain the IS auditor's involvement in system deployment or development.

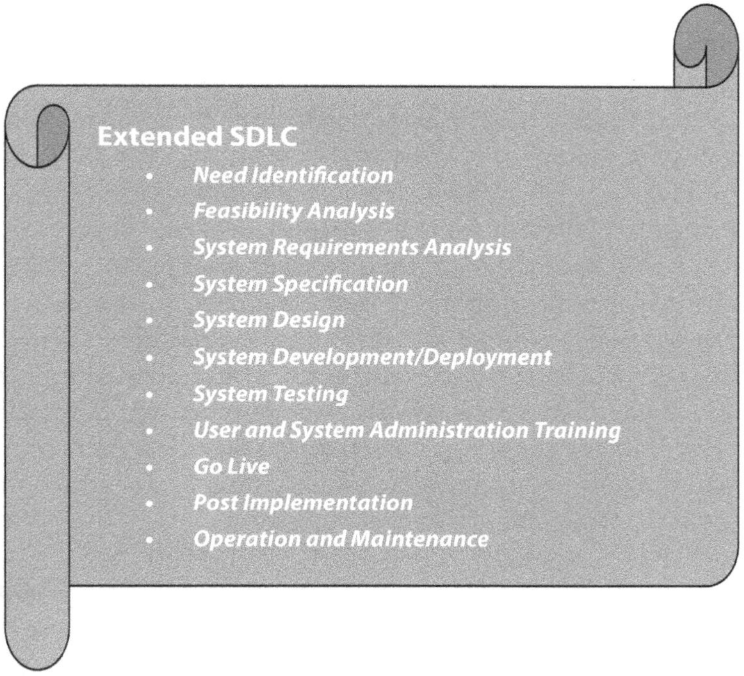

Figure 8.1 Extended SDLC

In order for the IS auditor to fully participate in systems deployment, it is necessary that they have basic project management skills so that they can keep track of various activities on the projects. Using project management software, the IS auditor will be able to have information on project tasks, duration, resources, costs, and dependences.

Need Identification

Enterprises have many competing needs especially if it is in a new market which is experiencing rapid growth and increasing product demand. These needs also include new information technology systems or upgrading existing IT systems. The initiation of such projects would be made by the user departments who are faced with a problem which needs a solution, might require implementing a new system or upgrading an existing system due to increased demand.

A good example would be a pension investment company which has been in business for over twenty years and has challenges with its current ERP system. The major problem being that the ERP system has limited functionality and most user departments are not able to expand on their services. Among some of the problems include inability to send alerts to customers, the database could no longer accommodate new customers, and the system was not web-based and could not be integrated with the new procurement system which was designed and developed in-house. Clearly there was a need which was identified by user departments in the enterprise. In some cases, the needs can be identified by the IT department or customers.

Once the need has been identified by the users' departments, the enterprise is required to set up a team which can explore the needs further and define the specific needs. It is possible that other departments might have other problems regarding the use of the ERP system or problems which are outside the current system which can be included in the new solution.

A good starting point would be for management to set up a team of users and IT department so that they can discuss the challenges they are facing with the current system and propose possible solutions.

At this stage, the IS auditor might not be directly involved in the discussion but will need to know the background to the current problems with the system. This could be done by being part of the team or indirectly through reading team reports or minutes. IS auditors also need to have the required understanding and knowledge of the enterprise in order to fully appreciate the problems the enterprise is facing.

Feasibility Analysis

A feasibility analysis involves a study of the viability of the proposal made during the needs identification activity above. The team appointed during the needs identification activity would explore the proposal further. The team will include users and IT department and possibly chaired by a senior member of management depending of the scale of the proposal. The use of a team is important so that the team can draw different ideas from across the enterprise. If the project affects the entire enterprise or a large part of the enterprise, it is recommended to use as chairperson a senior member of management who can not only represent management but also give the team the required influence and importance.

The feasibility will focus on the problems the proposal will address and how the team intends to address the problem, possible project costs, resource requirements, and the overall fit into the current operations of the enterprise.

The IS auditor should be part of the feasibility team in order to assist in the understanding of the requirements of the project and not to influence or have a say in the design of the system. Project background information will be important to the IS auditor as he prepares to take on this important role of advising, reviewing controls, security, and user requirements on the project.

The IS auditor can, at this stage, carry out preliminary investigations into what type of controls should be considered for the new system or what improvements to the control regime need to be included into the proposed system. The IS auditor can also look at controls in existing systems and what overall controls exist in the enterprises.

In order to ensure that the needs of the enterprises are taken care of, the feasibility team should look at the enterprise business strategy. The new project should not be in conflict with the business strategy but enhance its implementation.

The other area the team will look at is whether the new system will require introduction of new business processes or enhancing the current processes. This would be of particular interest to the IS auditor on how these new business processes will be integrated into existing business processes.

The IS auditor will need to review whether the feasibility analysis is also looking at how the new system will comply with the enterprise's IT policies and procedures. IT security policies and procedures are also of important concern to the IS auditor as these will be translated into security controls when the system is designed and deployed.

Operational requirements should be considered for the new system when conducting the feasibility study. The IS auditor should have a good understanding of the operations of the enterprise so that consideration can be made on the implications of introducing new systems or upgrading existing systems.

There are always important technical and administrative issues to be considered when introducing new systems. It is recommended that these issues are taken care of to avoid hiccups during implementation of the project. A good feasibility study will help unearth issues which need to be addressed and ensure appropriate analysis and conclusions.

System Requirements Analysis

After conducting a feasibility analysis, the team will have developed an idea of what type of system the users are proposing to deal with problems the enterprise is facing. The team is now tasked with the responsibility of determining what resources are required to implement the new system. The resources would include human, hardware and software, and financial resources.

Human resources include technical staff who will be involved in the designing, development, and implementation of the system. This will also include the IS auditor who will ensure that the system requirements are properly defined and meet the needs of the system to be deployed.

Hardware resources will include servers, workstations, networking equipment, and storage devices. Software resources would include systems such as databases, operating systems, utilities, and other supporting software. Each of these systems will need to be analysed in order to come up with specifications which will be used to procure systems which meet the proposed system requirements.

The enterprise might have its own internal standards which are used for defining system requirements. The enterprise might also use international standards for defining system requirements. It is important that standards are used as they help in determining appropriate standards for system requirements.

Financial resources are an important requirement which can be expressed in the form of a project budget. The budget should include the above indicated resources and other support services which would be required to successfully complete the project.

System Specification

This activity involves development of a specification which will be used to design a new system. A specification is a detailed blueprint of the proposed system. It is used to describe how the system will be developed, operated, and what type of technical resources will be required.

This is a very important stage as it also requires the IS auditor to assess the type of security and controls which have been proposed to be included in the system. The controls may include input, output, processing, and storage controls.

Input controls would include range checks, format checks, date checks, consistency checks, and other checks which can be used to validate data being captured.

Output controls also should be considered which address rights to access and produce output. Output authorisation might include output to hard copy or soft copy. Output controls might also include various categories of output such as read only, ability to read and write, access to summarised or detailed output, and many other ways of accessing information.

Processing controls are also included in order to ensure that data is processed according to defined requirements. There are various types of processing controls which need to be included in the system based on existing or proposed business processes.

Storage controls relate to controls on how data is stored and accessed. Databases normally have several inbuilt data storage controls. Other controls regarding data storage devices are environmental controls.

The IS auditor during this stage will be involved in reviewing the proposed controls and assessing how they meet the needs of the enterprises and the new system. The auditor will primarily focus on the specifications and proposed controls.

System Design

This activity involves the designing of the system. Using the system specification developed above, the development team will take up the challenge of designing the proposed system. The design is basically the structure of the system and how it will interact and integrate with other systems in the enterprise. The design of the new system would be based on the specification developed during the system specification stage. The project team during this phase will change character from a user-dominated team to a more technical team.

The development team might look at other options, either developing the system internally or hiring a developer. The team might consider customising an existing system used by a similar enterprise or one which closely meets the requirements of the enterprise.

The development team might also consider procurement of an off-the-shelf system which has been developed by software houses. Such a system should be reviewed by the development team to ensure that it meets the requirements outlined in the system specification. The IS auditor would also be interested in finding out if the system is able to incorporate the controls and security features outlined in the specification.

The IS auditor would look at a number of IT controls as the system is being designed. It is important that the IS auditor is involved in the design stage as the system is being developed and not wait until the development is completed. It is recommended that the IS auditor should review the system stage by stage. The development process should have a number of checkpoints and milestones. The milestone might be a completion of a module or sub-module. The IS auditor can review the development of the system after each milestone or checkpoint. The advantage of reviewing each module is that the development team will be able to rollback if the IS auditor raised issues which impact future modules or if there are missing system features in the developed modules. It is common to find system features which have not been developed accordingly to specification.

One of the critical controls which the IS auditor should review during this activity are access controls. These controls concern the rights of users on the system. The review will include reviewing controls which will be built into the system and those controls around the system. Inbuilt controls would include password controls, user account controls, and access rights to modules in the application system. Users will not have the same rights on the system, some users will have read-only rights, whilst others will have rights to post transactions and make changes to information stored on the system. Controls around the system will include authorisation of users to have access to the system and determining what type and level of access to be granted to various users and groups of users. In some enterprises, this process is conducted outside the system.

Processing controls are normally imbedded into the application systems. It is also the responsibility of the IS auditor to ensure that these controls are included into the system during the design. Processing controls would include procedures which enable processing of data as required by various business processes. For example, a business process might be used to pay commissions to brokers or sales representatives. A control can be designed which ensures that the right commission is paid by using the right commission rate, product type, and revenue generated.

Processing controls in some cases support complex processing systems and are also in themselves complex tools. Checking of all these processes require high-level skills and knowledge of system logic and possibly knowledge and skills in the platform and programming language which will be used to develop the system. The IS auditor can use various design tools which are available on the market. These tools can be used to test the design logic of a particular module or a set of modules. Other tools can be used to test data flows, database schema, and integration with other systems.

System Deployment

At this stage, the design of the system would have been approved by the development team and management. This stage is about developing the system. The development team has the option of developing a system from scratch or customising an existing system.

The development stage which involves coding a new system is normally used where the enterprise cannot find an existing system which closely meets the system specification or the enterprise prefers to develop its own system because of various concerns and requirements.

Development of a system can be time-consuming and complex. The developers will need to understand the design and specification of the system before they can start coding. The coding process itself can also be a long process, but with new technologies coming on the market, coding has been made easier with various modern and user-friendly coding tools. Developers nowadays have access to a library of development tools which include menus or dummy structures of application systems which can quickly be developed by addition of specific menus and other functionalities.

Internal developers can be used to develop the new system. This has the advantage of building on internal skills and experience.

The disadvantage is the cost of investing into development skills and also maintaining the developers after the project goes live. They might have to be redeployed or given additional assignments because there will be limited development work after the system goes live.

The enterprise can also choose to use external developers who have the required expertise to quickly develop and deploy a new system. External developers are normally dedicated developers with large investments in development tools and experiences.

Development of a system also requires the use of quality assurance specialists to ensure high quality is maintained. Testers will also be required to test the various code and modules which are being developed. All this might add to the overall cost of developing the system.

The enterprise can also opt to purchase an application system which is similar to what is planned for development and subject it to large-scale customisation. The enterprise can search for such an application system on the software market and involve the developers to customise the application system. This might be a faster way of deploying an application system without losing much time. Many software development firms are able to carry out extensive customisation in order to meet the requirements of the enterprise. Customisation has its own limitations as not all features can be customised as expected.

The role of the IS auditor at the development stage applies both to application development and customisation. The IS auditor is required to ensure that the application is developed accordingly to specification and should be involved in testing the application so that it meets approved system requirements.

System Testing

The system is developed over time and normally modular testing is conducted whilst system development is in progress. After system development has been completed, testing is required in order to ensure that the system is able to function properly as a unit. Testing would also involve users who would want to give the new system thumbs up before considering deploying the system.

During the testing phase, users would be involved in order to ensure that they are happy with the system and it does meet their expectation. Users normally have a good understanding of the business processes and should be able to assess if the system meets the business requirements. Users under the guidance of the testing team would use various techniques of testing the system. In most cases, it would be ideal for the users to perform walk-throughs such as data capture, printing invoices, processing transactions, and backing up data. Such walk-throughs would enable the users to appropriately comment on the functionalities in the system.

The IS auditor has an important task of testing the system to ensure that the controls are working as designed and are effective. The IS auditor apart from using testing tools might also be required to carry out walk-throughs, such as testing that access controls are working and the audit trail is capturing activities on the system as designed.

It would be important for the IS auditor, just as for the testing team, to develop testing procedures which would be used during testing. Procedures help to ensure consistency in testing the application system. Testing procedures should have been developed right at the beginning of the project or were already in the auditor's toolkit.

During testing, one important tool the IS auditor should insist on is ensuring the testing process is managed effectively through the use of change management controls. This tool enables the development team to manage all changes being made on the system. Once a test is conducted and an issue is raised, the test team will investigate further and conduct appropriate tests before making recommendations to the project manager. If the testing is accepted and approved, the change is implemented. Changes should not be implemented without the approval of senior management or the project manager. This ensures that there is consistency in the testing process.

Depending on what is being tested, the IS auditor will be required to have appropriate skills for the task. Lack of the right competencies might impact on the achievement of the testing objectives.

It has always been a challenge to find IS auditors with the right skills combination. It is often recommended to use other experts to complement the skills of the IS auditor. Using an IS audit team would be desirable as it would include auditors with various skills and also other experts with development skills in the platform being used by the software developers. Often it is not easy to find experts with the correct skills because software is sometimes developed for a particular enterprise only.

At the end of the testing process, a number of changes would have been identified and recommended. It would be up to the development team to assess how these changes fit into the new system and whether the project objectives are being met. It is possible that new changes might create new problems for the development team.

User and System Administration Training

Once the system has been developed and is ready for deployment, the project team might consider embarking on training users and IT administrators who will use and support the system. Training users is a key process because it can determine whether the system succeeds or fails. Users may point to lack of adequate training as the reason why they are not using the system after deployment.

Training for system administrators should also be conducted immediately after the system is ready for deployment as these are the specialists that will support the system and ensure that it is available 24/7.

The system administrators need to have thorough training and understanding of the system functionalities. They should be able to administer the system with minimum support from the vendors unless it is by design. The administrators also should be provided with properly developed system administration manuals. The administrators will require regular training updates so that they are able to support new releases of the software.

The enterprise should also ensure that they have appropriate service-level agreements (SLAs) signed with the software vendor or developer so that adequate support is provided.

It is often recommended that user training should be conducted at two or more levels. Before the implementation of the project, management should identify the champions of the project. Where there are many modules in the system, it is appropriate to have one or two champions per module. The champions will be responsible for the module and may also be the administrators of that module responsible for all user functions from training users, allocating user rights, recommending module updates, and monitoring the use of the module. The champions should receive a higher level of training than ordinary users.

Users should be trained after the champions have done their training. Champions can be involved in the training of users in order to give them an opportunity to develop their skills and have experience in the use of the application system. User training should cover all the required system functions or limited to a particular module allocated to a user.

In order to have an effective training program, users should have access to training manuals during and after training. These documents can be available through soft copy or hard copy. Online copies are usually desired as they are always available and consistent since they are regularly updated. Users in the course of their duties often would like to refer to procedures manuals. These documents should also be available online. When procedures change, these documents should also be updated immediately.

The IS auditor may not be a user of the system but is required to be trained on the functionalities of the system so that he is able to conduct effective audits. Where the IS auditor is required to conduct highly technical audits, more advanced training may be required by the IS auditor, which will include all the technical functionalities and supporting systems such as databases and integration tools. It is also a good consideration to have the IS audit team receive training on how to read and interpret data collected by reporting tools such as the system audit trails.

Go Live

After the system has been tested and the users have been trained, the next stage is to go live. The method of going live will really depend on the circumstances and requirements of the enterprise.

The enterprise might choose to use a parallel system or direct changeover implementation where the old system is dropped and completely replaced with the new system. Cost and availability of resources might be a factor in deciding which method to use.

Going live means that the users and management have signed off the project and they are ready for its use in the enterprise. The IS auditor, having been a member of the project team from start to this point, should also sign off and indicate satisfaction with the project and that it meets all the requirements as specified in the project goals statement.

It is important that the system has a rollback strategy. In the event of a major system failure or incidents affecting key modules, the go live can be aborted and rolled back to the old system. The IS auditor should ensure that this strategy is developed before the system is completely implemented. The rollback procedures should be properly tested and approved by the project team.

Documentation for the system which have been developed throughout the project should now be consolidated and updated where necessary. A number of things could have changed from the beginning of the project to this point and would include some key objectives. The changes need to be reflected in the documentation as they will be used for future training and for updating procedures.

The IS auditor should now be preparing for a new life. A project can be very involving and take a long period especially if it is a large system concerning a large number of users, customers, and in some cases, branch offices located in different countries.

The IS auditor should start at this point considering developing an audit program for the new application system. He might be required to develop audit objectives for the new application which the IS audit team should use to audit the new application system in the near future.

Post Implementation

The project team will require regular meetings to review operations of the system during the agreed period of post implementation. There is no standard duration of post implementation. The duration depends on the size of the project and complexity of the system. There could be many other reasons which might cause the enterprise to require a longer duration for post implementation.

It should be noted that despite the many testing activities and user involvement to review the new application system, some glitches might still remain and affect the post implementation of the system. The IS auditor will be required to review changes which are being proposed during post implementation.

If changes to the system are made during post implementation, the system documentation should also be updated to reflect the new changes. The documentation to be updated should include training manuals, procedures manuals, and any other essential online tools such as help menus or frequently asked questions (FAQ).

Operation and Maintenance

The post implementation period is usually of a limited duration, and often vendors would insist on a specific period. After the post implementation period, the system is considered to be in operation, and all systems should be monitored accordingly.

The IS auditor should also be ready to conduct regular application systems audits. We should remember that the IS auditor was not involved in the designing of the system but merely reviewing the various stages of the system development life cycle and ensuring that the required specifications regarding IT controls, security, and other relevant functions are implemented according to specifications.

Regular monitoring of the system by IT management is a required activity which would ensure that management is on top of things regarding the use of the enterprise application system. In some cases, monitoring tools might be embedded in the system and can be used by IT management to implement regular or continuous monitoring. The IS auditor would make use of the collected data during planned IS audits. The IS auditor can also use the monitoring tools to carry out regular or continuous audits.

During the life of the system, maintenance activities will need to be carried out, such as software updates, security fixes, and patches. The IT and user teams should put in place necessary procedures for handling system maintenance.

In order to ensure implementation of a good maintenance program, the enterprise should have a service-level agreement (SLA) with the vendor or software developer. The SLA can be used to ensure that the enterprise receives the required and appropriate service from the vendor. SLAs are contracts which can be difficult to implement in some cases due to different interpretations between the software vendor and the enterprise. It is important that both parties understand the requirements of the SLA by having meetings or involving other specialists before the contract is signed. The IS auditor should also be involved in the review of the SLAs and the IS auditors input would add value.

IT management should ensure that the source code is in the possession of the enterprise or an accepted escrow agent. If this is required, appropriate mutually agreed escrow agreements should be signed with the software developer. Where the enterprise does not need to keep the code, the IS auditor should advise management on the need to have a contract which will ensure that the enterprise can have access to the code in the event of the software developer going out of business.

The involvement of auditors in system development or deployment is considered a key requirement because it ensures that the system is developed or deployed according to agreed specifications. The role and responsibilities given to IS auditors during implementation of a system may vary from project to project. The key criterion is to ensure that the auditor is independent and there are no conflicts of interests.

CHAPTER 9

Auditing Disaster Recovery Management

Overview

Effective disaster recovery management is one of the critical requirements to ensuring that the enterprise is able to recover in the event of an incident. When planning for business continuity, the enterprise also addresses recovery of IT assets, such as hardware, software, data, and information. Recovery also includes human assets, such as skilled employees.

Many enterprises make large investments in disaster recovery which range from a few thousand dollars to millions of dollars. The level of investments depends on how critical the DRP infrastructure is to the business. In cases of large banks or stock exchange firms, the recovery of data is critical and can impact the business if recovery takes longer than expected. Most large banks and stock exchange firms operate in real-time and would set a recovery point which is very short possibly in seconds or minutes.

Implementing a disaster recovery plan brings a number of benefits to the enterprise, such as readiness to recover data and information in the event of an incident. An effective DRP also creates confidence in the internal and external stakeholders, such as management and business partners, on the reliability of the IT systems.

The IS auditor should be aware of the contents and requirements of major disaster recovery standards, such as ISO/IEC 24762:2008. There is also ISO/IEC 27031, a business continuity standard which can also provide valuable information to the IS auditor. Most disaster recovery plans are based on an international standard or an internally developed best practice standard.

A good starting point in auditing disaster recovery is by reviewing the disaster recovery plan in order to determine how it is being implemented in the enterprise. In this chapter, we shall focus on various activities relating to operation of a disaster recovery plan and the type of infrastructure required for implementing various levels of disaster recovery. We will also focus on various skills required in order to carry out an effective DRP audit and what type of evidence the IS auditor requires to collect during the audit.

IT Risk

The IS auditor requires a good understanding of IT risk. The IS auditor is required from time to time to carry out IT risk audits. Many enterprises are dependent on IT to run their business operations, and IT risk is one of the key considerations in the management of their operations. Management needs assurance that IT systems are able to deliver required services and that data and information is protected. IT should also add value to the enterprise in terms of growth, efficiency, and profitability.

Before we consider auditing disaster recovery, we need to understand what IT risk exists in the enterprise. A risk profile or register would be a good source of information on what risks the enterprise is facing and what mitigation has been put in place. In the absence of a current risk profile, the IS auditor might request the enterprise to carry out a risk assessment in order to have a good understanding of the risk exposure. In some cases, the IS auditor might carry out a snap IT risk assessment in order to have a general understanding of the risk environment assuming the client is agreeable to taking up the extra cost of the IS auditor performing a risk assessment.

A corporate risk policy should include an IT risk section where issues relating to disaster recovery are addressed. In today's business environment where many enterprises are dependent on IT, it is accepted that IT risk will always exist in the business and will change or take new shapes as the business grows or interacts with new business partners and introduce new products.

Enterprises interested in competing aggressively both on the local and international markets will be faced with the decision of adopting emerging technologies, which in many cases may not have been fully tested. The risk the enterprise might take is to use emerging technologies in order to have a competitive edge. Such technologies may fail and have a negative effect on the business or might succeed and bring in the much-needed revenues. The enterprise has to make a careful assessment before taking the risk of adopting new technologies or not.

Disruptive technologies are technologies which might introduce a new and cost-effective way of doing business. For example, electricity distribution companies all over the world supply electricity to factories and residential areas using copper cables. These factories and houses are connected to distribution hubs which are also connected to electricity generators. Scientists are currently researching on a new way of distributing electricity, such as using wireless devices. If the scientists have their way and they invent the technology for distributing electricity using wireless devices, this might prove to be disruptive on the business of electricity distribution. New companies might enter the industry and start distributing power more efficiently and cheaply using wireless technologies.

A carefully conducted IT risk assessment would identify various risks facing the enterprise, such as risk to the IT infrastructure, data, and information. It is important that the enterprise has a full understanding of the risk appetite as determined by the board and senior management. This information would help the risk team when designing and developing a disaster recovery plan.

Corporate risk includes various risks depending on the nature of the business and IT environment. The IS auditor should have a good understanding of IT risks before reviewing the disaster recovery infrastructure.

One of the risks facing an enterprise might be its inability to maintain critical customer services after an incident, such as a virus attack, a hacker breaking into the customer database, or an employee crippling the internal computer network. Inability to maintain critical customer services would mean that the enterprise may lose millions of dollars as required services would not be provided to customers. A prolonged outage might take the enterprise out of business or make it impossible for the enterprise to fully recover from the effects of the disruption.

Such an incident might also damage the market share, image, reputation, or brand of the enterprise. Competitors would also take advantage of the outage and offer customers alternative services. Customers would not wait for the enterprise to recover and restore its business. If customers discover that the enterprise is not able to offer services, they have the option of switching to competitors offering similar services. Such an eventuality would definitely cause the enterprise to lose its market share to competitors, which might be difficult to win back.

Most customers and suppliers might also suffer losses due to the disruption of services. This would result into the reputation of the enterprise being affected. Depending on how the incident is resolved, some customers and business partners might not be willing to take up new contacts with the enterprise. The brand would also suffer as it would be associated with a failed service. It would take time to repair such damage.

There is also the risk to company assets such as deliberate damage, natural causes, and theft. Deliberate damage to company assets can be caused by internal employees or external parties. It is common to see commercial espionage in certain industries where competitors initiate such actions of damaging assets belonging to other companies in the same industry. In some cases, damage to company assets can be caused by employees on industrial strike. They would deliberately damage company assets as a way of advancing their agenda.

Theft of company assets is another risk the enterprise faces. The company might have potentially lucrative assets, such as computer software, machinery, inventory, cash, and gold reserves. Such assets are a target of thieves trying to lay their hands on. We have heard of organized syndicates looting company assets on a big scale, such as processed minerals like gold or diamonds. Information is also a big asset in an enterprise which can be targeted by thieves and hackers who can later sell the information to competitors or other scrupulous agents. Information sits on enterprise servers which themselves can be a subject of attack. Hackers have become very sophisticated such that they are able to access information even in highly protected computer systems belonging to government departments and other large corporations.

Loss of company data and information can also be caused by malfunctioning computer equipment or due to poor maintenance work. Enterprises will always face this risk as long as they use computer equipment to support their business processes. Software can also fail if not properly maintained and monitored. Most known software failures are due to corrupted or improper configuration of software.

It is important that enterprises should also ensure that intellectual properties are protected. Enterprises face the possibility of losing intellectual property through theft. Intellectual properties include patents, trademarks, and copyrights. Criminals, through organized networks, can steal intellectual properties and use them as their own or modify the properties in order to use them as their own. Many enterprises have lost intellectual properties which they have later discovered being used by enterprises overseas. In the information technology world, we have seen heavy piracy of software. Many software developers have suffered financial loss due to heavily pirated software worldwide.

There is also the risk of losing human resources, and this can have an impact on the enterprise. Skilled human resources are key to the running of a business as they are the engine of the enterprise. Enterprises should ensure that the risk of losing key staff is taken care of and minimized, although it is recognized that employees will always leave the enterprise in one way or the other.

The other notable risk is the possibility of business control failure. This could result in the business not being able to run and control the enterprise as it interacts with other enterprises. Business control failure would also result due to lack of effective controls within the enterprise, which includes IT controls.

There is also a risk of failure to meet legal or regulatory requirements. The cause of breaching such legal and regulatory requirements could be lack of awareness of the requirements or deliberate non-compliance by the enterprise. There are many legal and regulatory requirements relating to information technology which have been enacted by many countries. Many of these are on IT controls and cybersecurity. You will also find laws and regulations on personal privacy and data protection requirements. IS auditors are required to have a good understanding of these laws and regulations so that they are able to effectively audit IT compliance in the enterprise.

Business Impact Analysis

Implementing a disaster recovery plan first requires that a business impact analysis is performed and the impact on the business is clearly understood. Business impact analysis is an assessment of the impact on the enterprise in the event that an incident occurs. After a risk assessment is performed, the next stage would be to conduct a business impact analysis. The analysis is normally performed by the enterprise risk management team or an external risk consultant. The IS auditor might also perform a new impact analysis if it will help in further understanding the risk environment and impact on the enterprise.

Impact on the enterprise can be rated as high, medium, and low. High impact, of course, has a devastating effect on the business. We earlier gave an example of an enterprise losing market share as a result of not being able to provide customer services because of a breakdown in IT systems. Medium impact might still have a disruptive effect on the enterprise. Measures need to be taken to ensure that the impact is reduced. Low impact may be acceptable to the enterprise as it is likely that the business may still continue with operations with minimum disruption.

It is important to take into consideration the cost of the impact. High cost to the business might mean that the enterprise might find problems in raising the necessary funds to recover operations if they did not put in place mitigation measures such as insurance.

Risks facing the enterprise can be rated as high, medium, or low depending on the type of risk and asset involved. The output of a risk analysis would include information on risk rating. Ratings would help analysts focus on high-risk assets and their impact. Risk assessment and treatment is covered in more detail in chapter 6.

In order to assess business impact in detail, it is important that we also look at classification of assets and operations. Classifying assets would help determine which assets are critical to the business. An enterprise makes use of various IT assets to provide the necessary support to the business. Below in figure 9.1, we have given examples of assets which could be critical to the enterprise. Let us take an example of a private university offering distance-learning degree programs.

#	Asset Description	Risk Rating	Criticality
1	Student Administration System	High	Critical
2	Payment Receiving Systems	High	Critical
3	Transport Monitoring Software	Medium	Non
4	Staff Catering Centre	Low	Non
5	Student Recreation Facilities	Low	Non
6	Examination Registration System	High	Critical
7	Student Counselling Centre	Low	Non
8	Internet Bandwidth	High	Critical
9	Faculty Reporting System	High	Critical
10	Network Servers	High	Critical

Figure 9.1 List of Assets

The IS auditor, when auditing disaster recovery, will be looking for evidence on how IT operations are being carried out in relation to disaster recovery. The IT function will provide various documentation including the disaster recovery plan for review by the IS auditor. It is recommended that the IS auditor carries out further tests by reviewing information generated by various disaster recovery systems and processes.

The disaster recovery plan is a good source of information when assessing whether the plan is working or not. The IS auditor would be interested in finding out if the DRP was approved by management, the composition of the DRP team, contact information for team members, recovery tests carried out so far, and if the plan is based on best practice such as an international disaster recovery standard.

Data Backup and Restoration

Enterprises, by virtue of their operations, generate and use vast amounts of data. This data is vital to the operations of the enterprise such that the data should be available to staff and customers all the time. Lack of availability of data could mean that the enterprise would not be able to provide the required services to its customers. In order to ensure that data is available in the event of a disaster, such as loss of data through deliberate deletion, disk storage corruption, or infection from viruses, the enterprise should put in place measures which will enable the enterprise to recover lost data in the shortest possible time.

One of the measures enterprises would develop and implement to secure data is to ensure that backup of data is done as frequently as possible and also having the ability to restore the data in the event of a disaster. Ability to restore data is as important as taking backups. An enterprise needs to ensure that procedures are in place for performing backups as well as for restoring backups.

There are different types of backup systems which enterprises can use. These range from simple copy and paste systems to large and complex backup systems used by multinational corporations. These backup systems have various levels of automation. Some backup systems are highly automated that they are able to take backups with minimum intervention.

In most desktop and server operating systems, you will find backup utilities which can be used to backup data generated by the operating system or application software. Backing up data using these applications would be from disk to disk, disk to tape, and disk to network resource or to the cloud. These are basic backup application systems which have limited features compared to commercial backup application software.

Backup utilities have a number of features such as being able to backup the system image only. In the event of a computer crashing, the system image can be restored. These utilities also allow users to set specific time and date when backups can be performed. This means that backups can automatically start even when the user is not available in the office.

There are also commercial backup applications which are used to backup large volumes of data in real-time. These backup systems are able to make backups of data on large databases over long-haul networks across countries or continents. These backups are taken as data is being captured using differential backups for example. Some backup systems use snapshots which copy data which has changed over a short period of time, such as a few seconds.

To prevent data theft, most backup systems have encryption features which protect backup data from being stolen or modified as it is transmitted over public networks, such as the Internet. Data can also be encrypted on disk storage in order to protect backups.

Error checking is one feature available in most backup systems. Data being backed up is checked for errors by comparing data being backed up with the source data. It is possible that data can get corrupted during backup or transmission. Where errors are discovered, a fresh backup is requested to correct the identified errors.

Backup software is also able to perform scheduling of backups. These allow backups to take place automatically without human intervention. The scheduler tools can be configured to run at a particular time and day. Several backups can be scheduled to run at different times. Many backup administrators would prefer to run backups in the night when the networks or servers are less busy. It is often a complicated situation when backups are done across different time zones to determine when and which location and networks are less busy.

Rollback management is another important feature in backup software as it enables the system to rollback in the event of an error. This protects previously backed up data from being completely lost.

Backup software support differential backup and incremental backup so that only data that is new or has changed compared to the backed up data is backed up. Most backup software have sophisticated backup techniques which are able to identify changes to data being backed up.

An enterprise should have in place a backup policy which will be used to support implementation of backup procedures. The backup policy is one of the documents the IS auditor would review before carrying out further audit work on the backup processes. Most of the information on backup processes can be collected from reports generated by the backup software or documents produced by backup operators.

Most online backup systems have inbuilt library controls which ensure that all backups are coded and documented. After each backup, the system will produce a report. A sample report is indicated below.

#	Description	Output Information
1	Backup Date	12-03-2014
2	Backup Time	09.30
3	Backup Type	Incremental
4	Data Origin	//Server01/data1
5	Backup Target	//server03/data1
6	Backup Completion Time	02.20

Figure 9.2 Backup Report

Most enterprises have off-site storage facilities where data is backed up. The off-site storage facilities are connected to the main office via networks using fibre, satellite, leased lines or wireless connections.

Off-site storage facilities should be secured so that unauthorized people do not gain access and tamper with data stored at the facilities. There are various security controls which can be implemented in order to ensure appropriate security at off-site storage sites.

Access to off-site storage facilities should be restricted to only authorised users with specific responsibilities at the off-site facilities. The authorization should be granted by management and regularly reviewed to ensure that access permissions to processing systems are appropriate. Access to the facility includes permission to physical security officers and those required to access and use the systems. Physical access controls can be implemented using swipe cards which are configured with appropriate access permissions. The enterprise can also consider use of different technologies such as biometric access pads which make use of fingerprints or eye retina.

Environmental controls are important as they ensure protection of systems and data from environmental hazards such as humidity, water, fire, heat, and power surges. The enterprise should provide the same environmental controls as those at the main data centre. The enterprise can, for example, install fire control systems at the off-site storage in order to protect the facility from fire hazards. Fire systems can range from the use of simple handheld fire extinguishers to automated fire suppression systems. The enterprise can also install surge protection devices which can be used to protect IT systems from power surges on both electrical power and computer networks. The enterprise can also install air conditioners which will provide cooling in the off-site storage to the required temperature. Servers produce heat which should be controlled in order to safeguard the equipment.

Where backup systems use tapes or disks, it is important that an off-site library control process is put in place. The library will consist of procedures for receiving backups, storing backups, and issuing backups when they are required. When backups are received in the form of physical disks or tapes from the main office, they should be recorded by the depositing and receiving officers and signed off. This could be a physical or electronic process. The same applies to storage of backups. The off-site administrator should have a system in place for clearly labelling the backups so that they can be easily located when requisitioned for use. The issuing process also should be documented and signed off by both issuing and collecting officers. This process will ensure that all backups are tracked both inside and outside the off-site storage facility.

Where backups are being made on movable disks or tapes, it would be expected that the enterprise would schedule backups at particular times or days to allow the operators to replace backup storage units. There are different types of disks or tapes in terms of storage space and loading mechanism. It should be noted that movable disks and tapes are no longer popular and are being replaced by online storage which is fixed in storage racks.

Whether the enterprise is using fixed storage or movable storage, it is a requirement that storage media is replaced with new ones after a period of use. The enterprise should come up with a policy as to when storage media should be replaced. There are many reasons why an enterprise would want to replace storage media, which includes increasing storage. Due to the ever-increasing volume of electronic transactions, an enterprise would find itself often running out of storage space if a proper storage strategy is not put in place. The other reason why an enterprise would require more storage space is the increase in the type of data being stored from simple text files to large graphical files. Enterprises twenty years ago would boast of having storage sizes of thousands of bytes. Today many large enterprises store billions to trillions of megabytes.

The other reason why an enterprise would replace storage is wear and tear of the disk mechanism and the magnetic material which is used to store data on disks. Technology may also be a factor as companies might opt to use new storage systems which are much more efficient and can hold large volumes of data.

Virtual storage is one other consideration, which is the pooling of physical storage from multiple network storage devices into what would appear as a single large-storage device. Storage virtualization software can be used to convert a server into a storage system. The software enables creation of large storage which backup administrators can use to perform backups of large volumes of data and data recovery more easily.

Virtual storage has been very useful in many enterprises which require large disk space but cannot afford the high cost of such systems. An enterprise can develop a storage area network which they can use to pool several storage devices on the network and use as a large single-storage unit. Enterprise networks have many computers with spare storage which is normally not used. A storage area network can be used to achieve this purpose.

Once backups have been taken, it is important that tests are performed to ensure that data can be restored. Enterprises are required to come up with policies and procedures on backup testing. More advanced backup systems are able to test data backups as backups are being taken. Testing restoring backups is still required in order to ensure that in the event of a disaster data can be restored.

Many enterprises develop test plans which are used to test backups and restoration of data. Test plans and procedures should be robust so that backups are fully tested. The IS auditor should review evidence on testing backups so that it can be confirmed that backups are being performed as well as testing backup restoration.

Recovery Strategies

Enterprises can implement recovery strategies in different ways depending on their needs and how they want to recover data and IT systems in terms of time, level, and point of recovery. High-level recovery strategies cost more than low-level recovery strategies. Choosing a particular strategy would depend on the assessment by the enterprise using a cost-benefit strategy. Figure 9.3 shows a pyramid structure of recovery strategies with those appearing on top being low-cost strategies.

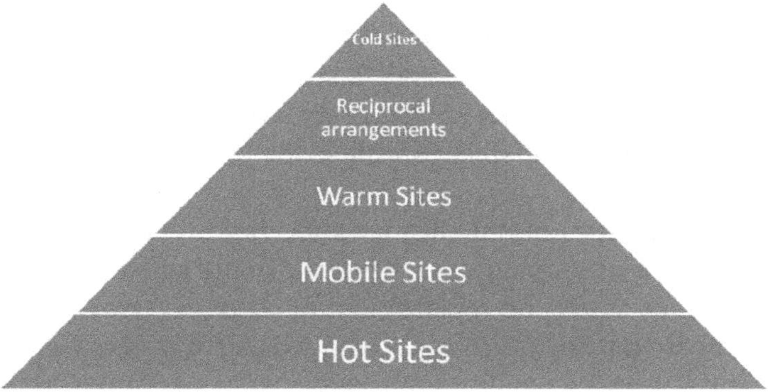

Figure 9.3 Recovery Strategies

Hot sites – This is a strategy where the enterprise provides a similar environment as the main data centre with all the equipment available such as servers, workstations, network equipment, and offices. The site might also have current data which is replicated to the hot site every few minutes or seconds. The environmental controls should also be at the level as the main data centre. In some hot sites, data may not be available and will be required to be loaded on to the servers before the users can make use of the facility. Ordinarily what should be missing are user connections. In the event of a disaster, all the enterprise requires is to get users to connect to the hot site and continue operations with minimum disruption. A hot site is basically a duplicate site of the original main site.

In most hot site environments, there are network connections which enable replication of data between the main data centre and the hot site. This allows the hot site to have the same data as the main site. There is also the requirement to maintain the same level of configuration of operating systems and application software. For example, the patches applied on the servers at the main site and hot site should be the same. This consistency will ensure that there is no software difference between the two sites.

The benefits of hot sites are that all systems are ready to be used when there is an incident. All users need to do is to connect or move to the hot site facility to continue work with minimum disruption. The time of recovery is short as systems are already in place. It is also expected that users would have received the necessary training and drills to work at the hot site.

The disadvantages of hot sites are that they are very expensive both in terms of keeping spare hardware, extra software licenses, maintenance costs, and replacement of absolute hardware if the equipment was not purchased using leasing. It is also expected that the enterprise would have to keep all equipment, software, and data up to date all the time so that there is no conflict of systems when a disaster is declared.

The IS auditor is required to review readiness of the site and that all the required equipment is available and users have been trained to operate from the hot site and do regularly rehearse working from the site. It is common to find users failing to find equipment at the hot site such as printers, scanners, or a standard office workstation environment.

Warm sites – These are sites which have hardware equipment such as servers and workstations installed and ready to be used. They also have network equipment and connectivity installed and ready for use. The warm site may not have current data as in a hot site. They might have backups such as disks or tapes which are a day or more old. The enterprise would have to enter into contracts with suppliers so that they are able to provide missing equipment at a short notice, but of course, this is at an additional fee compared to purchasing expensive equipment and software outright.

The benefits of warm sites are that it is cheaper to setup compared to the hot site as it does not have all the required equipment like that found in a hot site or main data centre. The warm site would have environmental control equipment in place such as air conditioners, fire suppression equipment, and power surge control equipment.

The disadvantage of warm sites is the time it takes to set up and move operations to the warm site. The enterprise would be required to install application software and transfer data before commencing business operations. The enterprise might also be required to install additional network equipment. The operating system software on servers and workstations might also require updating to match that which is on the main data centre.

The IS auditor would be required to review readiness of the site just like in the hot site and that all the required equipment is available and users have been trained to operate from the site and do regularly rehearse working from the site.

Cold sites – The cold site does not include any hardware and software already set up to operate. It only has limited facilities, such as electrical equipment and network cabling. Environmental controls equipment may be available, such as cooling and fire suppression equipment. The cold site does not include any data which has to be transferred on to the servers when installed.

The benefits of cold sites are that they have the least cost in terms of setup and a limited set of equipment is required. In a cold site, the enterprise also does not need to worry about keeping software up to date as these systems would be purchased at the point of need, such as when a disaster notice is activated.

The disadvantage of cold sites is that they would require some time to set up to full operation similar to the main site in the event of a disaster. Servers and workstations have to be procured from vendors, and this takes some time as many vendors do not keep stock of server equipment. It is possible that the enterprise can enter into contracts with vendors so that they can keep spare servers for emergency cases.

The approach the IS auditor would take is similar as indicated in the hot and warm sites. The level of preparedness in the cold site might be limited as only basic equipment would have been installed.

Mobile sites – These are sites which can be relocated to a recovery site for use. The mobile site could be a couple of mobile trucks with all the necessary computing facilities installed on board and can be moved to the operational centre within a short time to allow business to continue. Mobile sites are commonly used where an enterprise cannot relocate to a new site due to the need to have a physical presence in the area of operation.

Mobile sites are fully self-contained with diesel generators for power supply. The enterprise will have everything it needs to recover and continue with business operations on the mobile sites. The facilities will also have voice and data connectivity, servers, workstations, printers, and the required environmental controls.

The benefit of mobile sites is that the enterprise will have the ability to resume productivity following an incident without relocating to a new recovery centre and within a short time. Some mobile site vendors are able to provide mobile site facilities within an hour of a disaster. The facilities will have all the necessary equipment, software, and data to immediately commence operations.

The disadvantage of mobile sites is the cost of maintaining the contract. The contract will include the cost to maintain the equipment, software, and deployment of systems during a disaster. Since these mobile facilities are dedicated to a particular enterprise, the contract would include fees for maintenance staff and running costs.

Reciprocal arrangement – This is where an organization enters into an agreement with another enterprise with similar computing facilities to process data on their behalf. The enterprises should each have spare processing capacity, and in the event of a disaster, either enterprise can have their data processed by the other enterprise. In such a situation, either enterprise can reciprocate. The main requirement is that IT systems between the two enterprises should be similar so that only data is transferred to the other enterprise for processing.

The benefit of having reciprocal arrangements is that enterprises do not need to invest in extra facilities such as hot or warm sites. They also have available at their disposal systems which are similar to the ones they are using. Enterprises may charge a fee for use of the extra capacity.

The disadvantage of reciprocal arrangements is that enterprises need extra processing capacity to accommodate the other enterprise in the event of a disaster and this capacity might be idle most of the time. The other challenge is finding similar systems to the ones in use, especially in terms of software which has similar configuration.

Testing the Disaster Recovery Plan

The IS auditor is required to test the disaster recovery plan that it is effective and can be relied upon in the event of a disaster. The IS auditor will be required to collect evidence on how the DRP is being implemented.

One of the documents the IS auditor will need to review is the disaster recovery plan. The plan needs to be updated regularly to ensure that it's current and that it can be used when a disaster is declared. A plan which is outdated may be difficult to implement as some of the information contained in the plan may mislead the team. It is important that as the team meets at its regular meetings, any important change should be updated on the DRP document.

The composition of the DRP team is critical to the success of the plan and its implementation. It is expected that all critical areas covered in the plan should have representation from functional departments. The IT function should be represented at a high level in order to ensure that the plan is implemented with sufficient resources. Equally the line business managers should have representation on the DRP team.

Procedures for declaring a disaster should be clearly explained to all those involved in executing a recovery plan. A consistent approach by all involved is vital for the success of the plan. The enterprise is required to hold training sessions in order to ensure that the team is able to respond appropriately when a disaster is declared.

Communication is an important tool in the management and implementation of a disaster recovery plan. The enterprise should ensure that contact information for all members of the team is up to date and is constantly updated. Information for DRP team members should always be readily available, such as phone numbers, email addresses, residential addresses, and one or two social media contacts such as Twitter, Facebook, LinkedIn, and WhatsApp.

Practice sessions or drills covering various areas of disaster recovery should be conducted at periodic intervals. In some enterprises, drills are conducted once per year or more often where users need more preparedness to handle delicate disasters. Practice sessions should involve all key people in the enterprise including users who might be impacted by the disaster.

The IS auditor is required to document all his findings and advise management on the effectiveness of the plan. Auditing a DRP is quite an involving task and might require the use of more than one auditor to complete the task in time. The use of a project plan would help to ensure that the audit is properly managed.

CHAPTER 10

IT General Controls Audit

Overview

In this chapter, we will take a different approach in terms of presentation. We will use questions which normally you would find in an IT general controls audit questionnaire. Each question is followed by an answer focusing on helping you to develop evidence-gathering skills which are critical for an IS auditor to perform successful IS audits. It has been observed that many IS auditors do not pay much attention to the evidence-gathering process such that when it comes to analysing evidence collected during an audit, they find difficulties in reporting findings and conclusions which are well supported by evidence.

In order to make it easy to review various types of evidence which can be collected during an ITGC audit, the questions have been grouped into five sections. In each of the five sections, we will review five or more questions starting with IT governance. It is normally easy to use a questionnaire to collect evidence during an audit. An IS auditor can use questionnaires to conduct interviews with management. Preparing a set of questions in advance can be good practice as this will guide and help the auditor to cover all the necessary areas during an interview.

The IT general controls audit is performed in order to assess the level and effectiveness of controls existing in the IT environment. This is a high-level audit designed to give management a general understanding of the level and effectiveness of IT controls in the enterprise.

The ITGC is usually the first audit which is conducted before other detailed investigations are performed. Where controls are determined to be appropriate, the IS audit team can recommend that further specialised audits be conducted. If lack of controls is determined to be significant and material, the IS audit team may recommend that controls be improved before further investigations are done. A typical example would be a finding that all users are in the administrator group on an enterprise application system. This means that all the users have the same access rights and can perform all or any function such as reconfiguring the system, posting and reversing transactions, and making changes to data. This is definitely material weakness, and access controls need to be enhanced if the system has to be relied upon.

The ITGC audit can also be conducted as an independent audit to assess IT controls and security to data and IT systems. An ITGC audit gives management a general overview of IT controls and an assurance that data and IT systems are protected.

When performing an ITGC audit, a number of key areas can be reviewed, such as IT governance, IT risk, information security, information systems management, and IT operations. This is a high-level audit, and the IS auditor does not need to go into detailed investigations. His objective is to have a general understanding of the IT controls environment.

It is also important to know who the IS auditor will be interviewing before kick-starting the audit. Questions relating to IT governance are best dealt with by senior management or a member of the board. They should have a good idea of how IT governance is implemented in the enterprise. IT risk and information security questions may be handled by senior management. IT operations and information systems management would best be handled by IT management or system owners.

IT Governance

> It is recommended that an ITGC audit starts with IT governance so that the auditor can have a good understanding of how the board and management are handling IT issues. Where the board and management are not actively involved in IT issues, it is not likely that IT governance is properly implemented and that the board has got any significant influence on the use of IT in the enterprise.
>
> In this section, we will attempt to show how the IS audit team should investigate the level of IT governance implementation in the enterprise and collect evidence which will enable them to come up with well-supported findings and conclusions.

a) Have you implemented an IT governance framework in the enterprise?

The IS auditor would expect two responses from the client. One would be a categorical no or 'We have not implemented any IT governance framework'. Of course, some informal processes of IT governance might be in place without necessary management declaring that they have a framework in place. It would be useful for the auditor to make a follow-up by enquiring how the board and management deal with IT in the enterprise. Such a follow-up might give the IS auditor a hint of what is happening. If the enterprise has some form of IT governance system in place though informal, the IS audit team might recommend that management consider implementing a formal IT governance framework based on frameworks and standards such as COBIT, ITIL, ISO 38500, or other best practice recommendations.

In a situation where the client answers, 'Yes, we have an IT governance framework', this would be a good response, and the

IS auditor would follow up with a few further questions to help in collecting additional information and evidence to support the statement from the client. The first follow-up question would probably be to find out if the framework documented was approved by the board or senior management.

At this stage, the IS auditor would be required to request for a copy of the document with supporting evidence of board approval through minutes of the board or a written letter from senior management. Other supporting documents the IS auditor would collect as evidence would include an IT strategy document, IT policy, IT budget, and IT business plan.

You might have noticed that we have so far identified five important documents as evidence on IT governance from the first question. Other documents to be collected by the IS auditor would include the corporate governance framework document, IT governance procedure documents if necessary, and board minutes. A review of the documents would indicate the level of implementation of IT governance in the enterprise and the standard or framework which has been adopted by the enterprise.

b) Is the board aware of their responsibilities regarding IT governance?

It is possible that the enterprise could have an approved IT governance framework but the board might have limited understanding of their responsibilities due to poor implementation or sensitization of the board members.

If the response is in the affirmative, then the IS auditor should take note and find out if there are documents indicating an awareness workshop or implementation meeting which the board members and senior management attended. The IS auditor might also request that interviews be conducted with one or two board members to confirm this assertion. A review of board minutes might also provide useful evidence.

In this second question, the evidence the IS auditor would have identified and collected is a workshop attendance list, minutes of the IT governance implementation meeting, board minutes, and interview notes with board members.

If the response to the question was in the negative, the auditor would further investigate why this is the situation. Such information will help the IS auditor when making conclusions and recommendations.

c) How do the board and senior management ensure that IT adds value to the enterprise?

Assuming that IT governance has been implemented in the enterprise and both the board and senior management are aware of their roles and responsibilities, we expect the following responses from the client.

The response to the above question might be that IT does add value to the enterprise or it does not. Let's deal with the first possible response. If IT does add value to the enterprise, the IS auditor might want evidence how this is possible. The evidence which the client might point out includes increased efficiency and effectiveness due to implementation of new IT systems or upgrades. The client might also point to a new IT strategy plan which the enterprise has implemented. Increased revenue could also be one area indicating value from implementing IT in the enterprise. The human resource division might be happy to announce increased motivation in the enterprise and lower staff turnover.

If the response is that IT does not really add value to the enterprise, the IS auditor would be interested in knowing why it is so. It is possible that there could be no new investment in IT or the strategy is not appropriate. This finding will help the IS auditor provide to the client an appropriate recommendation on the way forward.

The IS auditor might collect different forms of evidence to support responses to this question. Where the response is increased investment in IT, the IS auditor would be interested in reviewing the financial statements and management reports for support to such a response. It could also be possible that a consultant was hired to assess IT service delivery in the enterprise after the huge investment in information technology. The consultant's report would be a valuable document in this case.

d) How do the board and senior management ensure that IT risk governance is properly implemented and managed in the enterprise?

It is expected that the board and senior management have a risk governance framework and policy in place which is used to guide implementation of IT risk. This is one way in which the board and management might ensure that risk is effectively managed in the enterprise. A risk register would be evidence that the enterprise has a good appreciation of risks the enterprise is facing. Regular monitoring of IT operations by management is also another way risk can be effectively managed. The IS auditor might request for monitoring reports to verify how the enterprise is managing IT risk. Meetings of the risk management committee would also provide good information on how IT risk is being managed.

Implementation of the enterprise risk policy by management includes executing risk procedures. Executing and adherence to procedures ensure that risk is effectively managed.

The IS auditor would be collecting the following information from the client: the IT risk framework, risk policy, risk register, minutes, and monitoring reports. The IS auditor should be aware that collecting these documents is not enough. Further review of the content is required to ensure that the information collected represents the correct evidence. IS auditing is not just a checklist job. It requires analysis of information if the IS auditor is to add value to the enterprise and enhance its performance.

e) How do the board and senior management ensure that IT controls are properly implemented and managed?

The board and senior management should have control over data and information produced by virtue of operations of the enterprise. Control over data and information is part of governance in the enterprise. In order to ensure effective controls, management needs to put in place a controls framework which will cover all areas of operations in the enterprise. Information is the lifeline of enterprises, and it is the responsibility of the board and management to ensure that control over information is effective.

If the response is positive and controls are properly implemented and managed, the IS auditor would request for more information to support this answer, such as checking for existence of controls, how the board ensures these controls are working through senior management, and how these controls are monitored.

As part of evidence-gathering, the IS auditor should have access to controls documentation and also reports on how the controls are being implemented and take note of weaknesses in the controls. IS auditors should take interest in investigating IT controls which are not properly designed and those which are not effective. This would help in coming up with findings and recommendations on how to improve effectiveness of these controls.

A review of the organisational structure of the enterprise would also help in assessing effectiveness of the IT controls in the enterprise.

If the answer is not positive, the IS auditor would ask further questions in order to find out why the board and senior management are not ensuring that IT controls are properly implemented and managed.

f) How do the board and senior management ensure that IT governance is properly implemented, monitored, and maintained?

The board and senior management should ensure that IT governance has been implemented at all affected levels. The board should ensure the IT issues are part of their agenda at board level. Regular reviews should be conducted by the board to ensure that IT adds value to the organisation. The process of ensuring effective IT governance would require that the board has effective IT strategies and policies in place and that management has the necessary resources to execute the policies.

Monitoring should be part of the process of ensuring that IT governance is successful and is adding value to the enterprise. This is achieved by regular monitoring through various assurances services. Internal IS audits can be regularly conducted to determine how IT governance is being implemented.

The board and senior management may also perform self-assessments which may help ascertain the level of compliance with IT governance processes. Self-assessments are beneficial in that the board is able to determine achievement of their own goals and give themselves a fair assessment.

It is also worth well to consider using external auditors or consultants to review IT governance implementation and maintenance. The frequency may not be as regular as internal IS auditors, but it is necessary to use external parties who might give a different or enriched opinion on the IT governance implementation processes.

The evidence the IS auditor would collect includes reports from auditors (internal and external), self-assessment reports from the board and senior management, management reports to the board, and reports from various stakeholders.

In order to collect appropriate evidence regarding this question, the IS auditor would be required to hold extensive discussions with the board and senior management of the enterprise in addition to reviewing various documentation.

IT Risk Governance

The board and management should have a good understanding of IT risk and how to mitigate these risks. The IS auditor will be required to collect sufficient information and evidence on how the enterprise is managing IT risk. Because enterprises are highly dependent on the use of information technology, IT risk should be rated as high risk. The questions used in this section are designed to assess IT risk and review what type of evidence an IS auditor would collect during an audit.

Assessing IT risk is critical to the operations of an enterprise, and it helps in determining how risks will be managed through implementing security processes and IT controls. Because enterprises are always experiencing change due to interaction with other organisations risk will also always change in various ways.

a) Does the enterprise have an IT risk management policy?

In big and well-established enterprises, the response would likely be in the affirmative. The IS auditor, as a follow-up question, would request for a copy of the IT risk policy. Other things to look for in the policy would be to check whether the policy was approved by the board or senior management and when it was approved. The IS auditor might also be interested in finding out if the risk policy is based on a particular risk standard, such as ISO 31000. This information would be useful when assessing the policy. It is important to note that in some enterprises, IT risk is implemented as part of the overall risk policy and not a separate policy.

If the answer is that the enterprise does not have a policy, the IS auditor should take note of the response so that he can include a recommendation in the report on the need to develop a risk policy. It would also be important for the IS auditor to find out why the enterprise does not have a risk policy and if there are any informal risk processes which are not documented. Informal risk processes would be a good starting point for management to consider in developing a risk policy. Information on informal risk processes can be collected by interviewing the board, management, and the other stakeholders.

b) What does the risk management policy include?

The risk policy should cover the enterprise end to end. The policy would address areas such as financial risk, operational risk, IT risk, business risk, unknown risk, and other risk areas. The other way would be to look at all the functions or departments in the organisation and try to assess what the risk policy should include.

The IS auditor would be required to review the policy in order to determine what is included in the policy. The use of a particular international risk management standard would be helpful in assessing what is or not included in the policy. Discussions with the risk committee or manager would help to gather more information on the policy and also help verify what is in the policy and what has actually been implemented. More important is that the IS auditor would need to collect evidence which will help in concluding that the policy includes all important aspects of the enterprise. This evidence can be found in operational procedures of various departments and how they handle risk procedures.

c) What standard has been used to develop and implement the risk policy?

The enterprise might implement a risk framework based on an international standard such as ISO 31000 or any other standards published by professional organisations. Enterprises can also develop internal standards which can be used to implement a risk framework. In order to ensure that the policy is based on best practice, the IS auditor should review the risk policy and determine the standard used to develop the policy.

The IS auditor should collect a copy of the standard used and the risk policy for further analysis. It is also possible that the enterprise could have used more than one standard to develop the risk policy. Enterprises are not restricted to using only one standard and can also include their own internally developed standards.

It is important that the IS auditor carries out some background research on the standards used. It is not unusual to find important updates which could have been released but not included in the risk policy for some reason.

d) What is the IT risk appetite of the enterprise?

The enterprise might decide to mitigate all the IT risks which have been identified by the risk team. In real life, it might not be possible to treat all risks. Management might also decide to accept some IT risks and hope nothing happens. These often are IT risks which have lower impact or financial cost is so high that management might decide to meet the cost of replacement if a disaster occurs. Normally enterprises treat risks in many ways. Insurance is one way of transferring risk.

Evidence on IT risk appetite can be obtained by interviewing the board or senior management. They have overall responsibility of managing risks and are in the best position to know the enterprise's IT risk appetite. Many enterprises with a formal risk function would document the enterprise's risk appetite.

e) What are the key IT risks in the enterprise?

There are many IT risks which might impact the operations of an enterprise, and through an effective IT risk assessment, the enterprise can find out what are the key IT risks. In most enterprises, IT risks may be the same, and in some cases, a few other risks may be specific to a particular enterprise depending on the nature of operations and IT systems in use. The IS auditor may be required to review the enterprise's IT risk register in order to find out what the enterprise has listed as possible risks.

Loss of data is a key risk since enterprises are highly dependent on IT and use information systems as their lifeline. Loss of data can be through theft by internal or external persons. Data can also be lost through damage to computer systems or malfunctioning systems.

There is also a risk of breaking the law, for example by not observing personal privacy laws. Management should ensure that staff are aware of personal privacy laws and develop internal policies and procedures which will ensure that these laws are observed.

Loss of information to competition is also a possible risk. Industrial espionage is common and can lead to competitors knowing about a company strategy and use it to their advantage.

The IS auditor should consider drafting additional questions as follow-up questions using the points listed above.

f) Does the enterprise have a risk management function?

An enterprise may have or may not have a risk management function. Depending on its size and type of business they are involved in, an enterprise may choose to establish an internal risk function or may opt to use external consultants.

Where a risk management department exists, the IS auditor may request for an outline of the functions of the risk department. The IS auditor will need to understand the role and function of the risk department especially regarding the development, management, and monitoring of risk. The auditor may also request for an organisational structure of the department in order to obtain an appreciation of the functions and control structure of the department.

The evidence required to be collected by the IS auditor includes existence of the risk function, roles of the department, structure of the department, and its relationships with senior management. The role of the risk management committee, if one exists, needs to be reviewed including its records, such as minutes.

The IS auditor should be mindful that the answers to the questions above are wide open and not limited to a yes or no response. The IS auditor should field a number of other follow-up questions in order to collect more information which can be used to support the auditor's findings and recommendations.

g) How is IT risk monitored in the enterprise?

It is important that management puts in place systems for monitoring risks in the enterprise. IT risk is always changing since enterprises exist and operate in a dynamic environment. If the response from the client is that the enterprise does have risk-monitoring systems, the IS auditor can request for further information on how IT risk is being monitored and what tools are used.

Procedures need to be put in place which all functions (including the board and senior management) will use to monitor risks. It is encouraged that the enterprise has a risk committee represented by all key functions in the enterprise which will monitor risks in addition to their other risk functions. In other enterprises, the risk committee is at board level with implementing committees at management level.

If the enterprise has no monitoring systems, this indicates that there is a serious weakness in the implementation of the risk framework. It is advisable that the IS auditor raises this issue with senior management.

The IS auditor will be required to collect evidence regarding monitoring of risks. The evidence would include reports from the risk management function, risk management committee, the board and senior management, various exception reports, audit reports, and data from risk-monitoring tools if any.

h) How does the enterprise ensure that members of staff are aware of IT risk procedures?

The response the IS auditor might get from such a question is 'Yes, we do regularly conduct risk awareness programs.' With such a response, the IS auditor will be expected to request for evidence which should confirm that the enterprise does have an awareness program and that it is operational.

The IS auditor might request for dates and where the awareness programs where conducted. He may go further and try to confirm from some individual users who attended these programs. What the IS auditor might be interested in is a standard awareness program which is consistent across the enterprise. It is also important to check whether people at various levels understand the IT risks the enterprise is facing and specific roles of members of staff in the risk management process. It is particularly important that this test is done at board, senior management, and operational levels.

The awareness program content should be consistent with enterprise risk policies and procedures. The IS auditor, as part of the evidence-gathering exercise, should request for the IT risk training program content which can later be analysed in order to assess if it is consistent with enterprise risk policies and procedures.

If the enterprise does not have any awareness programs for staff, then this is material for the auditor to report on. Risks affect all staff in an enterprise in one way or the other, and they need to be aware of the risks and how to respond to incidents which might occur. Risks are more appropriately managed if all staff are actively involved in risk management.

i) When was the last risk assessment conducted?

Enterprises do conduct risk assessments at regular intervals or when there are major changes to the enterprise IT or supporting systems. Enterprises also do perform risk assessments to less significant changes as part of change management depending on internal policies. Sometimes changes to less important system changes can cause major disruption to business operations. This is why it is important in some cases to ensure that risk assessments are performed even when less significant changes are made. Of course, we are not asking enterprises to perform risk assessments to every little change being made.

Management might give the IS auditor a standard answer to this question, such as providing only the date when the assessment was conducted. It is recommended that the IS auditor requests for a recent risk assessment report as part of the evidence and may go further by asking what actions management took in response to report findings and recommendations. You should have observed from this paragraph that the IS auditor can field two further follow-up questions which will enable him to collect a recent risk assessment report and a report on management responses and actions.

Information Security

Information security is one of the important and regularly audited areas in order to ensure secure and robust protection of the IT infrastructure. The IT general controls audit includes information security as one of the areas which are up for review. Generally the review will reflect what is contained in the information security policy and associated security procedures. IS auditors are required to investigate how security is being implemented and its effectiveness.

a) Has your enterprise implemented an information security policy?

If the client confirms existence of an information security policy, they should provide evidence in the form of a policy document which was approved by the board or senior management.

Approval evidence could be in the form of board minutes, endorsement on the original copy, or a letter from senior management. The IS auditor might further enquire by finding out if they are supporting security procedures which have been developed and implemented. Some enterprises maintain a separate security procedures document which is used by operational staff.

Implementing a security policy might in many cases require establishing a department to oversee the security function headed by manager or director with supporting security specialist staff. In smaller or medium-sized enterprises who cannot afford a full-time security department, they have the option of hiring external IS auditors or engaging one person to manage the security function on a full-time or part-time basis.

Where an information security policy has not been implemented, the IS auditor can recommend implementation of the security policy. In some enterprises, security is implemented in a piecemeal fashion and without a formal policy position from management. In this case, the IS auditor should still recommend that a formal policy be implemented to ensure robust and effective protection of data and IT systems.

b) What standard has the enterprise used to develop the information security policy?

It is important that information security is based on best practices, and there are many information security standards which have been developed by standards and professional organisations. Typical examples of security standards and frameworks include ISO 27001, ISO 17799, BS 7799, and COBIT for information security.

Usually the drafters of the policy document would indicate which standard the enterprise used to develop and implement the policy. Enterprises have the option to select only relevant areas of the standard to include. It is not a must that all areas in the standard should be included. This is because security requirements are not the same in all enterprises.

Some enterprises may opt to use internally developed standards. The IS auditor should request for such a standard and review it and determine if it meets best practice as recommended by international standards organisations.

It is unlikely that an enterprise might have an information security policy without using any specific standards. Where this is the case, the IS auditor would recommend a review of the policy so that it is based on an appropriate standard or other acceptable best practice document.

c) How does the enterprise ensure that all users are aware of the information security policy and procedures?

One of the requirements when implementing information security is to ensure that all users are aware of the information security policy and security procedures used in the enterprise. Information security is about everyone in the enterprise, not just IT staff, or management.

There are a number of methods which can be used to provide information security awareness training. The traditional one being regular workshops which are delivered via PowerPoint presentations, lecture style, or group discussions. Other methods would include use of online web technologies, podcasts, video, regular alerts, and bulletins sent by email or phone messages such as Short Message Service (SMS). Users can also attend awareness programs by completing online sessions which automatically email results to the training coordinators.

Information collected from the client should show evidence of users having attended awareness programs conducted by the enterprise. The IS auditor, apart from collecting evidence on awareness programs, should also assess effectiveness of the awareness programs. Users should be able to show that they understand information security requirements after the training. This information can be collected through interviewing users in selected departments.

From the explanation above, the IS auditor should be able to develop a number of follow-up questions which can be used to collect more detailed responses from the client.

d) Are there procedures which ensure that users are compelled to maintain confidentiality of company information?

The board and senior management should ensure that all employees sign a confidentiality agreement upon employment. This is an undertaking that company information will not be disclosed to unauthorised parties both within and outside the enterprise. Such a requirement protects the enterprise and compels employees against disclosing company information.

The IS auditor could request to perform a review confirming if all new joiners signed the confidentiality agreement. Some enterprises require staff to renew the confidentiality agreements every year. The existence of confidentiality agreements would be evidence that staff signed the agreements and are aware of this requirement. In other enterprises, the confidentiality clause is in the employee manual, and it is taken that once a new employee accepts employment, he or she also agrees to obligations outlined in the employee manual.

If the enterprise does not have a confidentiality agreement procedure in place, it would be the responsibility of the IS auditor to recommend that management implements such a procedure. In some countries, this requirement is a legal obligation, and all employees are required to sign the agreement especially in public organisations such as government institutions.

The IS auditor should be able to collect some copies of the signed confidentiality agreements, employee manual, and privacy policy in support of the positive response from the client.

e) How does the enterprise maintain personal privacy of customer data and information?

Maintaining privacy for customer data is a legal requirement in most countries. Most enterprises have implemented internal policies to ensure that personal privacy is maintained for customers and other information maintained for staff or suppliers.

Since it is a legal requirement in most countries, it is important that enterprises in such jurisdictions ensure that the board and senior management monitor implementation of privacy policy and regularly reviews its operation.

The IS auditor is required to collect evidence on how the enterprise is maintaining personal privacy requirements. A starting point would be to collect the company privacy policy and associated procedures. The IS auditor might also request for reports from staff responsible for implementation and monitoring of the policy. A review of these documents would give an indication how the enterprise is implementing the personal privacy policy.

Where a personal privacy policy is not available, it is again the responsibility of the IS auditor to advise the board and senior management on the need to observe personal privacy especially if it is a legal requirement.

f) What procedures do you have for granting access to IT systems on the enterprise IT infrastructure?

An enterprise should have access control procedures which require all users to be authorised before they can access IT systems. Access controls determine who can access the systems and what they can do on the system. Users are given different user rights depending on their job roles.

In order to access systems, users need to be authorised by their functional managers. This is a requirement in many enterprises and is a formal process where new or old users are required to sign access request forms whether manual or online.

The IS auditor can collect the access request forms as evidence and review them in order to verify that the procedure is being followed. The IS auditor should also check for evidence that user rights are regularly reviewed by system owners or managers. The IS auditor might also check the existence of dormant accounts and whether accounts for employees who have left the enterprise have been disabled or deleted.

If the enterprise does not have procedures for granting or denying access to systems, what would result is that users may have rights they do not need and may perform unauthorised activities on the systems.

g) On what basis do you grant user rights on an enterprise business system?

The basis for granting user rights is normally job roles or job description. Additional rights might be granted to users if they have extra responsibilities. If enterprises have a different method, they may find serious challenges as users might be given rights they do not deserve.

Evidence of what user rights have been allocated to various users can be checked by extracting user rights data from operating and application systems. The IS auditor may review the data by comparing user rights extracted from the systems with job descriptions.

h) What procedures has the enterprise put in place to ensure that data is recovered in the event of a disaster?

IT management might point to having implemented a disaster recovery plan as evidence that they can recover data in the event of a disaster. Enterprises should not only demonstrate that they have a plan but should also demonstrate that the plan that has been implemented is effective. Regular testing of the plan is recommended to ensure that data or systems can be recovered in the event of an incident.

The disaster recovery plan should reflect the requirements of the information security policy of the enterprise, and the IS auditor should review the document in order to ensure that the plan is consistent with the policy. There are various standards which can be used to implement a disaster recovery plan, such as ISO 24762.

Evidence the IS auditor could collect to verify the response from management includes the disaster recovery plan, test results of the plan, and the information security policy.

i) How has the enterprise ensured that the data centre is protected from unauthorised access?

Access to the data centre should only be for authorised persons. Authorised persons are those who have been formally authorised by management. Other persons can be authorised on a need basis, such as maintenance staff.

There are many ways of controlling access to the data centre, such as using lock and key, physical security, number locking systems, and biometric systems. Each system has its own merits and demerits.

Where the enterprise does not control access to the data centre, the IS auditor should report to management as this is a high-risk situation. The enterprise may not have proper records on persons accessing the data centre if there are no controls to accessing the data centre.

Evidence required to be collected by the IS auditor includes reviewing what locking systems are in use and any logs maintained by IT management to record who accessed the data centre over a period of time. If the enterprise is using electronic security systems, this information is automatically logged, and the IS auditor can extract this information from the application system used to manage access to the data centre.

j) Which environmental controls has the enterprise implemented to protect computing equipment in the data centre?

One of the requirements for the protection of computing equipment in the data centre is to ensure that an appropriate environment is implemented and maintained. This will ensure that the equipment in the data centre is protected from physical damage and secure from unauthorised persons.

There are many types of environmental controls which can be implemented in the data centre. The enterprise should ensure that the temperature in the data centre is controlled. This can be done by installing a cooling system in the data centre and operated at a recommended temperature. The enterprise can also install smoke detectors or fire extinguishers to protect the data centre from fire.

Where there are no environmental controls, the IS auditor should advise management on the need to have such controls.

The IS auditor might be required to make a visit to the data centre and conduct a physical inspection of the data centre. This way, the IS auditor would be able to have first-hand evidence on the environmental controls which have been implemented.

A visit to the data centre will also enable the IS auditor to ask several questions about the environmental controls in the data centre. Usually there are many controls which are implemented, and the IS auditor is advised to prepare a checklist which can be used whilst on a visit to the data centre.

k) What systems has the enterprise implemented to provide network security?

IT management should ensure that the internal resources on a network are protected from hackers or other unauthorised people outside the network. Hackers can also be internal, so when reviewing network security, this should be taken into consideration.

In order to secure network resources, different measures may be taken. Firewalls may be implemented and installed on the perimeter of the network. Personal firewalls may also be implemented on personal computers or laptops to protect workstations from unauthorised access by both internal and external hackers.

Enterprises that have not implemented network security are at risk of losing their data or having their systems damaged by unauthorised persons who could be motivated by personal or commercial reasons. The IS auditor should ensure management is aware of this situation so that corrective measures can be put in place.

It is recommended that the IS auditor should inspect the various security tools which have been implemented and assess their effectiveness. In addition to the firewall, the enterprise might implement security tools such as intrusion detection systems, CCTV, antivirus systems, and website security systems and antimalware scanners. It might be necessary to review configuration of these systems to assess their effectiveness.

l) What tools has the enterprise implemented for monitoring security of your IT infrastructure?

Security systems do not provide absolute security on their own. In order to support these systems, monitoring systems need to be installed. Usually these are automated systems which collect data from security devices such as firewalls and produce reports for analysis. Reports can show if certain malware or hackers are trying to access the network. Rogue network devices can also be used to access networks.

If an enterprise does not have monitoring systems in place, it is possible that they will not be alerted on unauthorised activities on their network. It is recommended that enterprises implement security monitoring tools.

The enterprise would provide a list to the IS auditor of security monitoring tools which they have implemented. The IS auditor, if he requires further evidence, can conduct a physical inspection to ascertain the installation of these systems. The IS auditor may also collect data generated by these security monitoring tools to ascertain their effectiveness. The IS auditor should also review monitoring reports to verify that IT management regularly use these tools.

Information Systems Management

Effective management of information systems is an important requirement if the enterprise has to achieve its objectives of being competitive and have an efficient service-delivery system. Information systems in this context refer to systems which are used in the enterprise to capture, process, and communication information via various types of reports. There are various types of application systems which are used in the enterprise, ranging from simple single-module systems to complex multi-modular systems, such as enterprise resource planning (ERP) systems.

a) Does the enterprise have a policy and supporting procedures for managing information systems?

The enterprise should have a policy or framework for managing application systems. Since application systems are the key tools for information processing in the enterprise, guidance is required on what type of application systems to implement and how they should be managed in order to ensure effective provision of support to business processes.

Where the policy and supporting procedures do not exist, the IS auditor can recommend establishment of the policy which should be approved by senior management.

The evidence the IS auditor would collect include the policy document and supporting procedure documents. User procedure manuals will also help to confirm that the policy is being actively implemented. Interviewing users and system owners would also help to assess if they understand the requirements of the policy and also its existence. The IS auditor can review the documents not only to confirm existence of the policy and procedures but to also assess if the policy meets identified standards or best practice recommendations.

b) Provide a list of key applications used in the enterprise

IT management would normally have an inventory of application systems used in the enterprise. The list would in some cases include functions of each application system. The drive towards using integrated systems such as enterprise resource planning (ERP) systems has reduced the number of single and non-integrated application systems in many enterprises. What is common nowadays in many enterprises is existence of a few integrated systems or a single integrated ERP system supporting all functions in the enterprise.

IS auditors would use the list as evidence of existence of application systems used in the enterprise. Where such a list is not available, the auditor might request IT management to prepare one before the end of the audit. The list can be used to select which application systems to audit if management has not indicated which systems to audit.

c) Provide names and positions of system owners for key application systems used in the enterprise

System owners are managers in the enterprise responsible for use and administration of application systems. It is important to know who the system owners are because they would provide invaluable information on how the systems are being used and managed. System owners are normally senior managers with functional responsibilities directly related to the application system being used by the department.

Information on regular positions or jobs of system owners is also important in that it will enable the IS auditor to assess the influence they have in the department and how they deal with internal politics or power play regarding management of information systems.

Management should be able to provide a list of names of system owners who can be interviewed later in order to collect more information on the use and implementation of the systems. It is common to find a situation where there are no system owners and all systems are directly managed by the IT function. In such a case, the IS auditor should recommend that the enterprise considers appointing system owners.

d) Are systems owners aware of their responsibilities?

System owners are given a description of their responsibilities when they are appointed to the role. The IS auditor should assess whether they know and understand their responsibilities.

If the response to the above question is yes, then the IS auditor should be able to collect the description of their responsibilities from IT or human resources department. In some enterprises, the role of a system owner is included in the main job description of the appointed members of staff.

If the answer is no, then the IS auditor should recommend to management that the job descriptions be officially written and distributed to system owners so that they understand their responsibilities and may be linked to annual employee performance assessments.

e) How do system owners ensure that data and information is secure?

System owners have the responsibility of ensuring that data and information is secure and protected. They normally work with the information technology security function to ensure that security procedures are followed and adhered to.

The IS auditor would be looking for responsibilities which show that the system owners also have security roles such as access control administration in the application systems. The reports which are produced by the system owners should also show that they have this role. Systems owners are required to report on security of data and information in their regular reports to management. For example, the system owner would be interested in knowing that the IT function does make backups of their data and that the data can be recovered in the event of a disaster. Where security incidents occur, the system owners should include such activities in the reports.

The IS auditor can also find more evidence by interviewing the system owners and reviewing security procedures related to specific application systems used by each system owner.

f) Who authorises user access to application systems?

The practice may vary from one enterprise to the other, but generally the line manager or system owners would authorise users to be granted access to an application system. Authorisation can be through any accepted method within the enterprise. This could be through signing a form which is in hard copy or electronic form.

Evidence can be obtained from previous authorisations made by the system owner or the line manager to confirm that procedures are being followed. IT department or system owners would normally keep copies of signed forms which can be made available to the IS auditor for review.

If the enterprise does not have such an access authorisation system or similar, the IS auditor should recommend that a suitable system is established and implemented.

g) How is segregation of duties applied in the application systems?

Segregation of duties could be based on job description. In the application system, this could be done by creating groups to which users can be added. Each group will have specific functions and rights.

The IS auditor can obtain evidence of segregation of duties by reviewing group functions on the system and individual user job roles. User rights can also be reviewed in order to determine specific user rights if they are not group based. The IS auditor should always be on the lookout for user movements, such as users who have left the enterprise, recently joined, and those who have moved from one department to the other. It's common to find that these users are still active on the system when they are no longer with the enterprise or are still holding old access rights when their job roles have changed. A good example would be an accountant who has been transferred to internal audit department. Definitely the accountant's user rights should have been changed immediately after the transfer was effected.

User rights can be complex in some cases and always changing. The IS auditor might be required to spend a bit of time auditing user rights, especially historical records related to some past activities performed by some users. This is common in high-volume transaction environments such as retail banks. Where the application systems are highly automated, the IS auditor can obtain most of the information online.

h) Are system patches and upgrades applied in a timely fashion?

System patches are technical or security fixes applied to operating systems or application systems. These are regularly made available by software developers such as Microsoft and Cisco. Some system patches are published more frequently than others.

It is recommended that system patches are deployed only after they have been tested by the IT department. Tests should first be performed on a testing computer such as a test server. If the tests are successful, the patches can then be deployed on the computers requiring the updates.

The IS auditor is required to review how quickly the system patches are applied by determining dates when the patches were made available and the date the patches were actually deployed. The IS auditor will also need to check which updates have not been deployed. This information can be obtained from the patch management servers such as windows server update services (WSUS) or system centre configuration manager (SCCM or ConfigMgr).

If the enterprise is using many application systems, the IS auditor would have more work of reviewing the various application systems. It is recommended that more time is allocated to reviewing test records and patching of application systems.

The IS auditor is required to ask a number of questions in order to obtain more information on patch management in addition to reviewing various testing procedures and confirming system patches which have been applied.

i) Are application systems in use supported by vendors or developers?

Application and operating systems should be supported by software vendors; otherwise, it would be difficult to use them especially when the systems have problems which require fixing by the vendor. Normally software vendors do not provide support such as providing patches if the application system is out of support. Vendors expect enterprises to upgrade their applications to new versions which are supported.

If the systems are not supported, the IS auditor can bring the issue to the attention of senior management so that the systems are upgraded or replaced. It is not advisable to allow a client to keep unsupported systems on their IT infrastructure.

The IS auditor can find out if the systems in use are still supported by checking with the vendor. This can be done by contacting the vendor by email or telephone. The auditor can also visit the vendor's website to confirm that the application systems are still supported.

Information Technology Operations

Management of IT operations involves managing and operating various types of hardware and software. On the software side, IT operations will involve running and maintaining operating systems at network and workstation level. This would also involve management and administration of various other application systems, which include ERP systems and single applications running on servers or workstations. In addition, the IS auditor will also come across software used to monitor and support other core systems running on the IT infrastructure.

The IT operations management team is also responsible for ensuring that hardware on which software runs is appropriately deployed and operated. Hardware includes servers, workstations, network equipment, printers, and other secondary devices which have been implemented in the enterprise's IT infrastructure.

The IT operations team also provides centralised services such as backing up data on servers and workstations and maintenance of all hardware in the data centre and computers used by staff.

a) Does the enterprise have an IT operations manual?

The IT operations manual describes various procedures used to run and support automated business processes in the enterprise. The manual might include the use of operating systems, application systems, network systems, telephone systems, and supporting systems such as disaster recovery procedures, systems monitoring, information security, and backup procedures.

Manuals would normally include detailed procedures which can be kept in manual or electronic form in a central location where all authorised users can access them. These manuals are essentially used to ensure that staff adhere to procedures when carrying out operations and minimize incidents of breaching procedures and expose the enterprise to various risks.

In big corporations, IT operations can be a huge operation with a large number of supporting staff. The work of the IS auditor might also require a good number of assistants to perform a meaningful audit.

The IS auditor would be required to test various systems on the IT infrastructure, and supporting evidence can be collected from IT operations activities such as operations reports, monitoring tools, online systems, and operations manuals used by IT operations staff. It would be important when reviewing the various documents and systems to focus on systems which are covered in the operations manuals. It is important that procedure manuals are up to date and can provide sufficient guidance to IT staff.

b) How does the enterprise ensure that IT staff adhere to operations procedures?

Adherence to IT operations procedures ensures that all work is carried out according to established procedures. Not following procedures could result in increased risk to the enterprise.

The enterprise can ensure that IT staff adhere to operational procedures by embedding IT procedures into business processes and insisting that all processes are conducted according to established procedures. Where there are no systems which ensure adherence to procedures, the IS auditor should report to management and make recommendations on the need to have such systems in place.

The IS auditor can obtain evidence from audit trails and other logs which record how systems are operated. Monitoring tools can also be implemented which can be manual or automated to help with checking use of IT systems. Physical observation is one other way the IS auditor can use to check adherence to procedures by IT staff.

c) Explain the enterprise procedures for IT change control management

IT change control is about ensuring that all changes made to IT systems are documented, tested, and approved before being implemented. Change control procedures ensure that change is managed and does not introduce new risks. Change procedures would involve generating a change request, designing the change, testing the change, and approval of the change before implementing it in production.

Evidence on the implementation of change control procedures can be obtained from change control documentation, which is generated as a result of implementing change control procedures such as change request forms, testing, and implementation documents. Where these procedures do not exist, it is recommended that the IS auditor advises management to take appropriate action.

d) What criteria are used to ensure that IT staff are trained in operating IT systems?

Training is a key part of ensuring effective IT service delivery in an enterprise. IT management should ensure that all relevant staff are trained to run IT systems efficiently. Trained members of staff have high motivation and perform better. All training programs should be based on training needs and related to requirements of IT systems deployment in the IT infrastructure. Most training on IT systems which have been deployed in the enterprise is conducted by vendors.

Information on staff training criteria can be obtained from the training plans, job descriptions, needs assessments, and actual training objectives.

The IS auditor can also interview members of staff on effectiveness of training attended. It is expected that after training, performance of staff should improve. Supervisors can be a good source of such information on staff performance.

e) What controls does the enterprise have regarding access to IT systems by IT system administrators?

System administrators normally access the systems using administrator accounts on application or network operating systems. The IT system administrators also can access the systems using their own personal accounts which have administrator privileges. Administrator accounts can be controlled by using access controls, such as granting or limiting rights for administrators, using password policy based on job descriptions, and monitoring the use of such accounts.

More information on administrator accounts can be obtained from audit trails and password and account policy settings on the IT systems. These settings are in some enterprises documented and can be found on the system. Data generated from monitoring systems can also be used as evidence for audit purposes.

f) How does the enterprise ensure that backups are taken and regularly tested?

A backup schedule should be developed and implemented which IT administrators can follow every day. Where backups are automated, the backup system should be configured to take backups as per schedule. A record would automatically be generated after the backup has been taken and can be reviewed by the administrator monitoring backup systems.

A test plan should also be developed which can be used for testing restoration of backups. Tests can be done at regular intervals as per enterprise IT policy. Evidence can be obtained from testing platforms and test documentation. The test plan should also ensure that there is a regular second test and sign off by the manager.

g) Does the enterprise have a maintenance plan for all IT systems?

Maintenance plans can be developed for both software and hardware. Plans can include dates, specific maintenance activities, duration, and resources required. It should be noted that major maintenance activities, such as upgrades, might require updating documentation such as procedure documents and system manuals. So a follow up question would be trying to find out if relevant documents have been updated due to system update or upgrade.

Lack of a maintenance plan can cause a lot of problems for the IT infrastructure such as not having timely maintenance works and having no budget and resources for carrying out maintenance.

The IS auditor can obtain evidence on existence of maintenance plans by requesting for the plans from IT department. The evidence should show how the plan will be implemented and which systems require maintenance over a specific duration. The IS auditor will be required to review the maintenance plans by comparing with actual maintenance works conducted.

h) Does the enterprise have service-level agreements with vendors?

It is essential that an enterprise has in place service-level agreements which will ensure that vendors are held responsible for the delivery of agreed services and quality of service. The enterprise is required to monitor the implementation of SLAs and ensure that they are timely renewed. A confirmation that the enterprise has SLAs in place should prompt the IS auditor to request for copies of SLAs for review. Obtaining copies of SLA is evidence that agreements do exist, but the auditor should also check that the SLAs are valid and that the dates have not expired and they are duly signed. The IS auditor may be required to ensure that the SLAs are properly drafted and do include the required service scope.

Absence of SLAs means that the enterprise cannot hold vendors responsible for any works which are below expected standards or which are delivered late.

i) What procedures do you have in place for monitoring IT systems?

In order to ensure that systems run 24/7 the enterprise should make sure that systems are in place for monitoring operating systems, application systems, servers, network equipment, telephone systems, and other systems which have been implemented by the enterprises. Lack of monitoring systems would result in having systems which suddenly stop working without warning. Where systems are monitored, administrators can use dashboards to monitor systems which are in production and produce timely reports. The systems can also be configured to send timely alerts to administrators to facilitate prompt action.

IT management would provide a list of monitoring systems they have in place. Typically in highly automated environments, the IS auditor would find a single dashboard used to monitor all systems used in the enterprises.

The evidence the IS auditor would obtain includes a list of monitoring systems and associated procedures used to support the systems. Data generated by the monitoring systems can be used as evidence that the systems are working and have been implemented. The IS auditor can also use the data to assess if the monitoring systems are working efficiently and providing correct data.

CHAPTER 11

Application Systems Controls Audit

Overview

Enterprises regularly conduct application systems controls audits in order to give assurance to management that application systems are able to produce correct information which can be relied upon and used for decision-making. Application system controls (ASC) refers to the use of rules and procedures to ensure completeness and accuracy of data.

Data integrity and validity is one of the key objectives of application systems controls audits, and IS auditors are required to test data integrity and validity using various methods and tools.

The application systems controls (ASC) audit can also be conducted as an independent audit to assess controls and security in an application system. An ASC audit gives management a detailed assessment of IT controls and an assurance that data is secure and protected.

Enterprises deploy application systems to automate business processes, and in many cases, the IS auditor will find complex application systems which have been designed to accomplish high-end business tasks using large volumes of data such as big data. It is important that these processes are checked regularly in order to ensure that they produce accurate information for business decision-making. It is also especially important to carry out checks when changes are being made to the system whether they are one-off or routine changes.

ASC audits are often conducted after IT general controls audits have been completed and a positive assessment of controls is reported. Where there are material weaknesses, the ASC audit might be delayed to allow management to address the issues raised by the IS auditors during the IT general controls audit.

ASC audits are also conducted as independent and specialised audits due to the high complexity of some application systems which are used to capture and process billions of megabytes of data and, in some cases, across large geographical areas.

There are many examples of application software which are used in enterprises ranging from simple administrative applications to large systems used in production, research, banking, and airline ticketing systems. In office environments, the IS auditor might find the following application systems in use:

1. accounting software
2. customer relationship management software
3. asset management software
4. payroll software
5. human resource software
6. enterprise resource planning software.

In this chapter, we will focus on one key audit activity which is evidence-gathering just as we did in chapter 10. We will look at how to collect evidence and what type of evidence to collect which is relevant to an ASC audit. I have observed that many IS auditors do not pay much attention to evidence-gathering such that when it comes to analysis of information collected, they find difficulties in reporting findings and conclusions which are well supported by evidence.

In order to make it easy to review various types of evidence which can be collected during an ASC audit, we will use a question-and-answer format. In this chapter, I have included six sections which we will use to review application controls. I have added two additional sections which you would not normally find when reviewing application controls but are necessary in order to have a complete review of application controls. I have included database controls because databases are normally firmly integrated with application systems and a review of database controls is therefore essential. The second inclusion is application systems integration controls. In most IT infrastructure, the IS auditor will find application systems which produce output which is automatically used by other systems as input. In other systems, the input is done manually but with less efficiency. Integration and interoperability between applications is a common feature in modern application systems, and it is important that IS auditors review controls around system integration.

It is easy to use a questionnaire to collect evidence during an application systems audit. An IS auditor can use questionnaires to perform interviews with management or other suitable methods such as observations or system interrogation. Preparing a set of questions in advance is good practice as it will enable the IS auditor to cover all the necessary areas during an interview.

It is also a good idea to arrange interviews with appropriate members of management who can provide authoritative information. Questions relating to application system governance are best dealt with by senior management or system owners. Senior management should have a good idea of what is expected and how application system governance is implemented in the enterprise. Application system operations issues would best be handled with by IT management or system owners.

Application Information Systems Governance

Application information systems governance involves the use of application systems to automate business processes. Application systems are a lifeline of an enterprise dependent on the use of information technology. Application information system governance is part of the overall IT governance in the enterprise.

Application information system governance directly involves business users who use application systems on a day-to-day basis. The IS auditors will review the organisation structure around the management and use of application systems, maintenance of the systems, security of data, relations with vendors, IT department, and other external parties using the system.

It is recommended that an ASC audit starts with governance so that the IS auditor can have a good understanding how management, system owners, and IT are handling application system governance and management. Where management is not actively involved in IT issues, it is not likely that governance will be properly implemented and that management has got any significant influence or control on the use of application information systems in the enterprise.

The IS audit team should investigate the level of application system governance implementation in the enterprise and collect evidence which will enable them to come up with well-supported findings and conclusions.

a) Who are the system owners for the ERP system and what formal positions do they hold in the organisation?

A large application system such as an ERP would normally have a system owner and champions. A system owner would be someone in senior management with direct supervision over business processes which use the application system or ERP.

The IS auditor would be looking for information on how the system is managed. Evidence the IS auditor would be looking for includes names of system owners and champions and formal positions they hold in the organisation apart from being system owners or champions. The IS auditor would review meeting minutes and other documentation to establish whether management and system owners are actively involved in the management of the application systems. This information will enable the auditor to access whether there is a governance and management structure over the application systems.

It would also be important for the IS auditor to further investigate if performance of system owners and champions is also assessed based on these additional roles.

b) Does the implementation of the ERP system form part of the IT strategy which is aligned to the enterprises business objectives?

The IS auditor will be trying to assess if the enterprise's IT strategy is aligned to business objectives. The enterprise might not achieve its business objectives if the two are not aligned and each one would be pulling in a different direction. The ERP system implemented by an enterprise should directly reflect how the enterprise wants to achieve its goals.

The evidence can be collected by reviewing IT and business strategies and objectives of the ERP system which has been implemented. The IS auditor can also interview senior management to validate information found in IT and business strategy documents. Observing how the system is being used in the enterprise would provide further information on whether the ERP system is helping the enterprise achieve its objectives.

c) How does the enterprise ensure that application systems enhance the efficiency of the business operations?

Application systems are used to automate business processes so that delivery of services is enhanced. Automated business processes enable faster, effective, and efficient provision of services to customers. There is also lower operating costs and higher quality of service when business processes are automated. Enterprises can ensure that efficiency is introduced in the business by implementing IT systems. It is important that application systems address the requirements of the business if efficiency and effectiveness is to be accomplished.

Evidence on the enhanced efficiency of an enterprise can be obtained by interviewing senior management and finding out their views on business performance after introducing the systems. IS auditors can obtain evidence by reviewing historical data on performance relating to costs, service delivery, and utilization of human resources. Return on IT investments can be another way of assessing automation of business processes.

d) Does the enterprise have an application systems maintenance plan?

An enterprise should have a maintenance plan in place which will be used to ensure that application systems are updated according to the agreed plan with the vendor. Patches to the software in use should be done timely so that security issues are addressed as they are identified. Maintenance also includes fine-tuning the system to meet increased capacity demand by the enterprise.

For example the system might need more hard disk capacity to handle increased data needs or upgrading the processing unit so that the system is able to handle more complex processing requirements.

The IS auditor can request for a written system maintenance plan which was approved by management. The IS auditor may also seek more information on the performance of the plan by reviewing what has been implemented and what is outstanding. Usually the IT department would have documents which have been signed off showing maintenance works which have been accomplished. The IS auditor should keep in mind that the documentation being collected should be reviewed so that appropriate conclusions and recommendations can be made.

e) Does the enterprise have service-level agreements (SLA) with vendors who implemented the application systems?

Service-level agreements are contracts between an enterprise which has purchased or implemented an application system and a vendor who supplied the software. The SLA tries to ensure that the vendor provides services according to agreed parameters and standards. If the vendor does not adhere to the provisions of the agreement, the vendor suffers penalties as outlined in the agreement.

It is likely that IT management would say yes, they do have SLAs with all or some of the vendors. In the event that there are no SLAs, the IS auditor would recommend to management to consider putting in place SLAs to support the application systems. The IS auditor should seek further information whether the SLAs have been implemented and are being observed in terms of performance. The SLA documents should also be duly signed by both parties.

The IS auditor may interview managements in both the client and vendor organisations in order to find out how the SLAs are performing. The IS auditor may also review the SLA agreements in order to find out if the agreement protects the enterprise.

The IS auditor would collect SLA agreements, performance reports, and notes from interviews with management. These documents should be reviewed by the IS auditor in order to extract information which can be used to make conclusions and recommendations to management.

f) Do you have change management and security policies to support application systems in use?

Change management policies and procedures ensure that all changes are tested, approved, and documented before being deployed into production. Change management helps reduce risks which might result from making changes such as upgrades, applying patches, and fine-turning systems.

Information security policies are implemented in order to secure data and information resources from accidental or deliberate damage by hackers or internal users. Security involves various other procedures such as access controls, protection of information assets, disaster recovery, and network security.

Enterprises should have change management and security policies in order to guide how changes and information security is implemented. IS auditors can request for policy, procedure documents, and various operational reports which can be reviewed in order to assess how the policies are being implemented in the enterprise. Policy documents can be obtained from IT department or other departments responsible for assurance services.

g) When did the enterprise last perform a risk assessment covering all key application systems?

Risk assessment enables an enterprise to determine its risk exposure. Enterprises can identify risks or update its risk profile by performing risk assessments regularly. Risk assessments can also be performed when changes are being made on IT systems. IS auditors are required to appraise themselves with risk management policies and procedures of the enterprise so that they can conduct effective application systems audits.

It is important that a risk assessment plan be developed which can be used to conduct regular risk assessments or when there are new changes to be implemented. The IS auditor would be interested in knowing when the last risk assessment was conducted and the reasons why the risk assessment was performed. The IS auditor can also review all other relevant changes in order to determine that risk assessments are performed when changes are being made.

Evidence of whether risk assessments are regularly performed can be obtained from risk assessment reports, departmental reports, or management reports and meeting minutes.

Input Controls

Input controls are used to ensure that captured data is accurate, complete, valid, and consistent. Various types of input controls are used, which are either automated or manual. Automated controls are embedded in application systems. Input controls are important as they enable the enterprise to have clean data. Clean data will enable the enterprise to have accurate reports which can be relied upon and used for decision-making.

IS auditors should conduct input controls audits in order to determine that the design of the controls is correct and that the controls are effective. Examples of input controls include input authorisation, data validation checks, input error reporting, batch controls, and use of transaction logs.

a) Are automated input controls supported by manual methods?

Automated input controls are in some cases supported by manual methods such as the use of manual source documents. Hard copy receipts and invoices can be used to capture data into the system. These documents could contain control information such as receipt numbers, account numbers, and cost centre codes.

The IS auditor should have detailed information of these manual methods so that he is able to assess what controls are used. Often errors might originate from these manual source documents, and the IS auditor can recommend that changes be made to the source documents in order to eliminate persistent errors.

The IS auditor can interview managers and various users in order to ascertain what manual methods exist in addition to performing walk-throughs, observations, and reviewing procedure documentation.

b) How does the application system ensure that input data is complete?

Input data can be captured from source documents which have similar data requirements as on-screen forms. The application system input form can be designed in such a way that it will only accept input data if all fields are filled in. If the form is submitted with some fields not completed, the system will reject the form and send an error report or highlight fields which are not complete.

The auditor can test such controls by performing a walk-through on a test server. Control documentation can also be reviewed to determine how the controls operate. Where such input controls do not exist, the IS auditor can recommend to management that appropriate controls are designed and implemented.

c) How does the system ensure data accuracy?

Application systems use input controls such as validation checks to ensure that data being captured is accurate. An example would be the use of date validation which will have an embedded control with a date format such as dd/mm/yyyy. This control will ensure that only data which is in date format is accepted. An additional control can be included which will be used to check the input data for a specified range such as a date which falls in a particular range like a year or month.

The IS auditor can collect evidence on data accuracy by performing data analytics on captured data. The IS auditor can extract data from the system and compare with data on source documents. The IS auditor can also perform walk-throughs to test input controls.

d) What control procedures does the enterprise have in place for input authorization?

The enterprise can use access controls to authorize users to input data into the system. Authorisation can be granted based on particular types of input forms or data. For example a user may be authorised to input cash transactions but cannot input invoices from suppliers. Access control procedures are normally written for reference by users and administrators. The IS auditors can review these procedure documents to test existence and effectiveness of these controls. The IS auditor should regularly review user access rights which have been allocated to users on the application system. This will give the IS auditor sufficient information on input authorisation activities.

The IS auditor can go further by conducting reviews of authorisation documentation which were used to grant input authorisation. Authorisations could have been done manually or on the system. Activity or audit logs normally would record creation of user accounts and allocation of user rights which IS auditors can use to review input authorisation processes.

e) How is segregation of duties implemented?

Segregation of duties allows users to perform specific functions on the system. The roles are determined by job descriptions or job roles. In some cases, users are granted extra duties in addition to their everyday job roles. Access rights are also applied to groups which will consist of users with similar job roles.

The IS auditor can review segregation of duties by comparing allocated user rights with job descriptions. User rights can be found on the application system or offline documentation. Job descriptions are usually available with human resources department or line managers.

f) How does the system handle input errors?

Application systems generate error reports after a batch has been captured and submitted. In other application systems, error messages are displayed on-screen once an input form is submitted. The system highlights all fields with errors. Users can then make changes to the input data and resubmit the form. There are many other ways in which input errors are handled, and this varies from one application system to the other.

It is recommended that IS auditors conduct walk-throughs to test if error-handling controls are effective. Walk-throughs would include inputting test data and reviewing the results. Enterprises also do maintain error-handling procedure documents which IS auditors can use when reviewing implementation of error-handling procedures.

g) What controls does the application system have for data captured using website input forms?

Systems which are available on the public networks such as the Internet face a lot risks from hackers and other unauthorised users. Enterprises should take extra care to ensure that such systems are secure. Most online input forms use web tools and sit on servers which are not on the internal network. Once data is submitted, it is temporarily stored on servers which are not on the internal network. Captured data is validated including checking authorised data sources with valid accounts; the data is then sent to the main servers for processing. Other systems handle online input data differently using more complex procedures. The IS auditor should review what security controls are used on the websites such as transport layer security (TLS) or secure sockets layer (SSL).

The IS auditors can conduct a walk-through on online systems to test effectiveness of the controls and also to confirm if the design of the controls is appropriate. The IS auditor should check online forms to confirm if they conform to documented online data capture procedures.

h) What controls does the enterprise have for data transfer between systems?

Output from one system can be directly used as input into another system. Such systems are very efficient as there is no need to re-enter data. Because of the automated input system, it is important that data validation processes are able to check for errors accurately and reports generated to alert users. It is also important to note that once errors are captured into an integrated system, all other modules will pick the same errors. Transaction logs are useful tools which can be used to check for input errors. IS auditors can also be used to test effectiveness of such controls.

ERP systems are one such example as they do have several modules. Data captured in one module can be used immediately as input in another module. A request to purchase a motor vehicle from procurement department will enter into the system as input into the procurement module. After processing, the output from the procurement module will go to the finance module as input without any further manual intervention.

Processing Controls

Processing controls are used to ensure that data is processed according to established rules and that the results produced meet expectations. Processing controls are built inside the application system and all data used by the application is processed based on established rules. Examples of processing controls include run totals, verification of amounts, comparisons, checking account status, logical operations, and use of key field controls.

a) How does the system ensure that internal processing produces the expected information?

Application systems process data which is stored on databases and produce information in form of various types of reports. Internal processing converts data into information using defined instructions or codes, such as adding numbers, subtracting dates, importing, and adding totals from another file. These instructions are preconfigured in the application system. Correct configuration of application systems is important in order to ensure that they produce accurate information. If a script used by an application system is not correctly programmed to calculate commission, the results of processing will always be wrong. It is the responsibility of the IS auditor to ensure that configurations, scripts, and other programming functions are checked for errors through regular audits.

Auditors would confirm that processed data is correct by comparing input data and output information using analytical tools such as Excel, ACL, IDEA, or other advanced tools.

b) Does the system produce transaction logs?

Most application systems produce transactions logs which are a record of transactions taking place on the application system. The transaction log would record the date the transaction took place, the amounts involved, the ID of the user, reference code for the transactions, and other relevant information. This information is very useful to both the IS auditor and the user as it has all the details of the transactions. The transaction log can be used to track transactions taking place on the system.

If the application does not produce transaction logs the IS auditor should take note and report to management. The IS auditor should request for a copy of a transaction log from IT department or system owner for review.

It would be useful for the IS auditor to take a sample of data in the transactions log and test it for errors or unauthorised activities.

c) How is access to data on databases achieved?

Access to the database is through a user account which was created by the database administrator. In some applications, the user account on the application system is mapped to the database account or group account and uses permissions defined on the database when accessing data. Where user accounts on the application system are mapped to group accounts on the database, the IS auditor will be required to review the account mapping in order to make sure the mapping was done correctly.

The IS auditor can review access rights on the database to determine what type of rights have been allocated to user and group accounts. The IS auditor may be requested to audit user accounts or group activities on the database.

d) How does the system process commissions for sales consultants?

The application system would use a commission business process to compute commissions for the sales consultants. In the application system, an automated process for paying commissions can be used to process commissions. When the commission process is selected from the menu and input variables identified, commissions are processed and a report is produced showing all commissions to be paid to the consultants. The variables would have been captured into the system such as sales amounts, commission rates, and product type. The application would use this information to calculate commissions. The application system uses data stored on the database in addition to other variables which are captured at time of processing commissions. In other application systems, scripts are developed and used to process commissions.

The IS auditor should try to establish what controls exist for processing commission. This information can be obtained from the application system itself, commission payment processes, scripts, and by interviewing sales managers or staff in charge of such processes.

e) How is processed data stored?

Processed data refers to information mostly in the form of reports or other output which have been produced after data has been processed. Processed data can be stored in hard copy or soft copy form. Soft copies are stored on storage devices such as internal or external hard drives. The IS auditors are interested in knowing how information is protected and secured in the enterprise. Unauthorised disclosure of information may affect the enterprise negatively.

Enterprises do have policies on how information is stored and protected. The IS auditor can review these policies and also check how the policies are being implemented. Such information can be found by reviewing security controls in application systems and how output is handled.

f) How are business rules applied on application systems?

Business rules are developed in order to regulate how business transactions are conducted. Business rules are configured into the application system and determine how business transactions are processed. Business rules are important controls as they help regulate business activities.

ERP application systems are complex systems with several business rules covering all functions in the enterprise. IS auditors should pay particular attention on how these rules are applied and relate across business functions.

The IS auditor is required to review application of business rules so that it can be determined if they are applied properly and support business processes effectively. Evidence about application of business rules can be obtained from application systems documentation and by interviewing business managers. The IS auditor can also perform walk-throughs to observe how the application systems process data into various forms of output.

Output Controls

Output controls are used to ensure that access to processed data or output is controlled and only available to authorised users. Output can be produced in many forms which include output on computer screens, output in hard copy, and output to other application systems which is used for further processing.

Enterprises do not want to have their business activities exposed to competitors and will do everything possible to secure data and information. In recent past, we have seen big enterprises having their client data being stolen or hacked into by unauthorised users.

a) How does the enterprise ensure reports are protected from accidental or deliberate disclosure?

Output can be protected by using access controls which will grant access to only authorised users. Unauthorised users cannot view or print output which they have no authority to access. Production of output such as printing can also be limited to selected printers. Information security awareness programs can also be conducted regularly so that employees are aware of the need to protect information from unauthorised users both internal and external to the enterprise. Such measures can ensure that output is protected from accidental or deliberate disclosure. Measures also need to be put in place to protect information which is in hard copy or voice form.

Evidence on whether the enterprise is appropriately protecting output can be obtained by reviewing access controls on output and storage of information. The IS auditor can also interview users to obtain an understanding of how they protect information and if they are aware of policies and practices on information protection.

b) What control procedures does the enterprise have in place for output authorization?

Users are authorised to produce output in either print, on-screen, or both. Management can decide depending on a user's job role to grant appropriate access to output. For example management might decide that only front office staff should have authority to print cash receipts. The responsibility for authorising access to output is with line managers or other designated officials.

The IS auditor can review access control documentation to check user access rights on the system. Further evidence can be obtained by checking access control configurations on the application systems.

c) Which reports are restricted from users who are not managers?

Management will from time to time decide which information should only be available to managers and not accessible to non-managers. Such decisions can be made depending on the sensitivity of information being handled. Management reports for example can only be available to managers.

The IS auditors can review access rights to determine who has what rights to reports. Access can be granted based on job roles or at senior management discretion.

Everyone can have access to management reports if the enterprise does not have restrictions. The IS auditor would recommend that restrictions be applied depending on the policy of the enterprise.

d) What control procedures does the enterprise have in place for output distribution?

Output can be available for distribution by email, printing, viewing online, or download. Distribution of output should be controlled in order to ensure that unauthorised people do not have access to it.

The IS auditor can obtain information on output distribution lists from senior management. It is recommended that the IS auditor interviews users and managers in order to find out if the controls are working or too restrictive thereby stifling business activities.

e) What controls does the enterprise have for printing sensitive documents?

Depending on organisational policies on access to information, sensitive data can only be accessed by managers and others who have been given specific rights due to their job roles or additional responsibilities. A typical example would be payroll data. Only the payroll manager and his staff may be given rights to print the payroll and payslips. Because this is sensitive information, only specific members of staff will be given rights to print payroll information.

The sources of information on such controls include access rights on the payroll application system and specific printing rights on the print server. This information can be found by checking the access rights configuration on the payroll application or documentation prepared by IT department or system owners.

f) How does the enterprise ensure that output is kept confidential?

One way in which users can be made to keep output information confidential is by getting them to sign a confidentiality agreement. The users should clearly understand the requirements of the agreement and consequences of not observing the agreement. In some enterprises, users are required to renew the agreement every year.

The other way is by using access rights which restrict access to output to only authorised persons. We have referred to access controls in most of the questions above which is an effective way of ensuring that access is restricted.

The IS auditor should review confidentiality agreements to determine if all employees have signed the agreements. The IS auditor can also review various management and privacy incident reports to check if users are observing confidentiality. It is often not enough to just check who has signed the agreements, IS auditors are also required to check how the agreements are being enforced.

Data Storage Controls

> Data captured using the application system is stored on internal or external storage. Data stored on storage systems require to be protected from unauthorised users and from physical damage. Storage systems are themselves also subjected to environmental controls to ensure that they are protected from environmental hazards.
>
> In this era of big data, the need for sufficient storage to enable various types of data analytics is high and ever increasing. This also means that the enterprises need to apply extra measures to ensure that data storage devices are protected and effective controls are applied.

a) How is access to data stored on external backup storage granted?

Access to external backup storage and backup systems require special access rights normally reserved for systems owners and administrators. The practice may be different in other enterprises who might grant access to certain users or to IT staff only. Backup data is stored on external storage which can be accessed online or by manually loading data from external storage media. Data can also be kept on large virtual storage servers and users will not notice the difference.

The IS auditor will require evidence that there are controls on how backup data is accessed and how access to backup data on external storage is granted. Authorisation will normally be granted on a need-to-know basis. As in other answers above, evidence can be obtained from access control data and other documentation on access rights maintained by the enterprise.

b) What procedure does the enterprise have for ensuring data integrity?

Data integrity involves ensuring that data is protected from accidental or deliberate modifications by implementing input controls, processing controls, change controls, and data storage controls. These controls can only be effective if they are properly designed and regularly monitored by both management and other internal stakeholders.

In an enterprise, control procedures are developed to ensure data integrity and IS auditors should be able to review these procedures by checking documentation and the controls embedded in the application system. It is recommended that control procedures should be documented in order for employees to use and implement the procedures effectively. Documentation can also be used by IS auditors to test effectiveness of controls.

c) How often is application data backed up? And is a record of backup activities kept?

Management will develop backup policies and procedures which are used to keep backup data for use in the event of an incident. The frequency of data backups depends on many factors such as the sensitivity of the data, frequency of updates, volume of transactions, and type of backup to be performed. There are many methods of backups such as full backups, partial backups, and preferential backups which can be performed.

A record should be kept to indicate when backups were taken. A record can be kept on a manual or automated system. Most automated backup systems do keep an electronic record after backup. IS auditors most often want to confirm that backups are being taken by checking backup records. It is also good practice for internal control purposes that management has access to such records.

d) Does the enterprise test backups? If yes, how often are backups tested?

Good practice demands that backups be tested to ensure that data can be recovered in the event of an incident, such as data corruption, hard disk failure, or loss of data through theft. All tests should be documented so that a record is kept for future reference. The frequency of backup tests depends on how frequently data is updated and the volume of transactions. Where the volume of transactions is high, the enterprise might need more frequent tests. However, the policy on backups largely depends on IT risk. If management thinks the risk is high, backups can be performed more frequently.

Information on backup tests can be collected from backup test records which IT administrators keep after performing backup tests. These records could be manual or electronic depending on the level of automation in the enterprise. If the enterprise does not keep a record of test backups, the IS auditor should take note and report to management.

e) Does the enterprise have a data protection policy?

Most enterprises do have data protection policies which are used to protect personal and corporate data. Employees are required to have a good understanding of data protection regulations as most countries have legal requirements for data protection.

The IS auditor should review the data protection policy in order to ensure that it meets the requirements indicated in the data protection act. It would not help even if an enterprise had a data protection policy if the policy does not meet the requirements of national laws on data protection.

The IS auditor should look for information on how effective data protection policies are in the enterprise by looking at statistics on violations and also by interviewing management in order to find out how effective the practices are. The IS auditor should obtain a copy of the policy as evidence of existence of the policy.

One other related and important requirement is the personal privacy legislation which has also been enacted by many countries. Enterprises are required to ensure that personal information is used only for purposes it was collected unless they have specific authorisation from their customers.

f) Has the database been security hardened?

The installation of a database system is normally a default installation with many services enabled even if they are not required. A number of security features are also disabled by default. In order to harden the security of a database, the administrators are required to disable any services and ports not required by the enterprise and enable required security features in order to enhance database security.

The IS auditor will be required to review the security implementation of the database and any supporting documentation. The review will include conducting a walk-through on the database system in order to verify all security settings.

Application System Integration Controls

> Most enterprises do conduct business with many suppliers and customers, and due to the automation of many business processes, they find themselves in a situation where they need to integrate their business IT systems in order to enhance efficiency and processing of transactions.
>
> Integration of IT systems require implementing of controls which will ensure that data going in and out of one system to the other is protected, valid, and consistent. Integration of IT systems running on different IT infrastructure can be very challenging to implement.

a) How does the ERP system connect to external application systems?

Most application systems implemented in enterprises are required to connect and send output or receive input data from external systems operated by suppliers or customers. In this case, the integration could be enabled by middleware software which sits between the two systems.

Both enterprises should have documented integration controls ranging from access controls, VPN connections, connection protocols, and data transfer procedures.

The IS auditor should be able to review these interconnections in order to ensure that both enterprises are protected. Depending on the size of the enterprises and volume of transactions, the integration process might be complex and require detailed SLA agreements to implement.

b) How does the enterprise ensure that data transfer between your ERP and other systems is controlled?

Control of data transfer is done by first establishing connectivity through the virtual private network (VPN); the second phase would be for the application systems to perform a handshake and allowing actual data transfer.

The VPN connection can be reviewed by checking the configuration on the firewalls, routers, or other devices which are used to create the connection. It is important to check the connection information generated by the devices to ensure that the connections are correct and secure. The handshake between the application systems should also be checked. The statistics can be generated by the middleware software or the application systems by posting details in the transactions logs.

It is advisable that the IS auditor apart from reviewing the controls should also review sample data to ensure that the data passing between the two systems is valid. This can be done by extracting sample data and testing it using data analytics software such as Excel, ACL, or IDEA.

c) What are the major risks of integrating systems?

The major risks could be security as the systems reside in different locations and managed by two different enterprises. The two enterprises should regularly monitor the performance of the two systems in order to ensure that they function correctly and data is processed through without being corrupted. The other risk is systems malfunctioning and bringing operations to a halt. A fallback system should be put in place in the event of system failure.

The IS auditors should ensure that the enterprises do regularly conduct risk assessments in order to ensure that integration risks are managed.

d) How would the enterprise ensure that data transferred to external systems is accepted?

The middleware software will handle the handshaking, data transfer, and ensure that data transferred is accepted. The systems will also use a common protocol to ensure easy identification of data.

The IS auditor can review logs being generated by the middleware software or application systems to validate the data exchanged by the two systems. A regular review by the IS auditor is essential in order to ensure there is data integrity and consistency.

e) Does the enterprise have written procedures for supporting and implementing application systems integration controls?

Once the integration is established, documentation needs to be produced, which will be used to support operations of the systems. The IS auditor should review the documentation in order to ensure that the systems operate according to approved controls and procedures.

f) How often are integration controls reviewed by internal auditors?

Integration controls should be reviewed more regularly and implementation of automated monitoring systems would help to ensure effective operation of the systems. The IS auditor should also perform reviews of the integrated systems in order to ensure that controls are effective and procedures are being followed.

CHAPTER 12

Specialised Information Systems Auditing

Introduction

Specialised IS audits are performed to support other types of audits, such as IT general controls or application system controls audits covered in chapters 10 and 11. A typical example would be an Oracle database audit. We are referring to such audits as specialised because they require a special approach and skills which are beyond a non-specialised IS auditor. Oracle database audits would be conducted by other experts according to 1204.1 ISACA IT audit standard. The 1204.1 (using other experts) standard requires IS auditors to use other experts where they do not have the necessary skills and competencies to conduct the audit. For example, if the IS audit team does not have oracle database skills, they may not be able to carry out the audit which will meet the requirements and standard expected and achieve the agreed engagement objectives.

In this book, we have categorised all audits other than IT general controls audits and application controls audits as specialised audits. Of course, one might be tempted to say that application systems audits can be called specialised audits because they require working knowledge of the application system. Such audits may be called specialised audits if they do not take a general approach but also require the use of technical knowledge and skills in that particular application system. For purposes of differentiating between the three types of audits, we will look at specialised audits as a different type of audit which requires technical understanding of an application system. Examples would be ERP systems such as SAP, Oracle, or Sun Business System.

In this chapter, we will review a number of audits which fall under the description of specialised audits. Our focus will be to review key areas which should address audit objectives of specialised audits.

Types of Specialised IS Audits

We will review IS audits which we are calling specialised audits so that the IS auditor can have a good picture of how these audits are performed. There are various objectives of performing specialised audits, and many depend on the client's requirements and operational demands.

Information Security Auditing

Information security involves the securing of the enterprise's IT infrastructure and protection of data and information. A lot of resources are usually expanded to provide the necessary security in an enterprise ranging from network security systems, security servers, and employee security awareness training. Enterprises with a keen interest in securing their systems do implement information security policies, standards, and procedures. In large enterprises, you will find a formal information security organisation with a number of employees specifically charged with the responsibility of implementing, monitoring, and reporting on information security to management.

Information security not only provides protection to data and information but is also an enabler of business. Where information security is properly implemented, the enterprise is able to provide services in a secure manner which not only protects its business activities but also its customers and employees. An enterprise stands to benefit by receiving return business opportunities if customers feel protected and can conduct transactions in a secure environment. Of particular importance nowadays is the issue of privacy. Customers take privacy very seriously and will always want to get assurances on what the enterprise is doing to protect their personal data.

Audit objectives describe what the client wants the IS auditor to perform when carrying out an IS audit. Often during information security audits, the client might want the IS auditor to test system security in the enterprise or test performance of the security infrastructure. Audit objectives might also be highly technical and require an IS auditor to test the design of the security architecture in an enterprise, for example, reviewing how security is managed on the stock exchange with real-time functionality and connected to other stock exchange systems around the world.

Sometimes audit objectives may be general or only require the IS auditor to perform compliance tests with information security policies and procedures. Such audits are fairly standard and may not require specialised skills. Such audit work can easily be handled by a general IS auditor on the team.

There are many security standards which can be used to perform information security audits or to guide in the development of information security audit programs. Common security standards include ISO 27001, ISO 17799, and BS 7799. ISACA has also published COBIT 5 for information security which addresses a number of security areas. The IS auditor will also come across many other proprietary security standards or frameworks published by vendors which are specific to operating and application systems.

In a specialised audit, the IS audit team will not only use audit checklists and questionnaires but will also get to use specialised security audit software when performing the audit, such as penetration testing software, data flow testing software, antivirus and antimalware software, security monitoring tools, intrusion detection software, and many other such tools.

The challenge of auditing an information security infrastructure is that every day there are new threats as the enterprise grows, evolves, and find new opportunities of conducting business. The IS auditor, just as the information security teams, must always be on the lookout and ensure that they are abreast with new developments in information security. The security team should always be on the lookout for new security risks, threats and vulnerabilities. On the other end, hackers are also in action, trying to find new ways of penetrating systems of governments and enterprises.

Information security is a specialised field, and it is recommended that audit teams make use of experts in this area. This is particularly important if the audit objectives are specific and require a detailed and technical security audit. Securing high-end systems which are used to manage operations of large enterprises with millions of customers require specialised skills.

Computer Forensic Auditing

The ever-growing incidents of computer crimes being committed around the world has also led to the increased demand for services from computer forensic specialists. IS audit teams regularly make use of computer forensics specialists to investigate computer crimes. The specialists join the IS audit team as other experts.

Computer forensics involves the use of special investigation techniques to collect evidence from computer systems where crime has been committed. Forensic specialists use special software tools to carry out investigations and preserve evidence. The evidence obtained by the forensic expert is used by the IS audit team to support their audit findings, conclusions, and recommendations.

The audit objectives of a computer forensic audit are developed to ensure that evidence is collected to support findings from the IS audit team. The IS audit team might find that there is possibility of fraud having been committed. In order to have a strong case, the IS audit team would request that other experts investigate the case further using forensic techniques. The audit objectives given to the IS audit team and the forensics expert would generally be the same. What would differ are the techniques used to collect and preserve digital evidence.

Computer forensic standards have been developed by International Standards Organisation and other professional associations to support forensic work. The suite of forensic ISO standards includes ISO/IEC 27037, 27041, 27042, 27043, and 27050. ISACA has also developed guidelines on carrying out computer forensic audits.

The evidence collected by forensic experts has been regularly used in courts of law, and the experts are required to follow standard procedures of collecting and preserving evidence. In many countries, laws have been enacted which should be followed in order for evidence to be accepted in a court of law. Many best practices have been developed worldwide which are used to ensure observance of forensic investigation procedures.

Computer forensic experts make use of various tools to investigate crimes committed on computer systems. Some of the tools include MailXaminer used for collecting evidence from 20+ mailbox formats, WindowsSCOPE used to analyse a computer's volatile memory, and Forensic Explorer (FEX) used as a multipurpose computer forensic tool.

The major challenge of computer forensics is ensuring that evidence is not contaminated or tampered with. Computer forensics specialists and enterprises involved in computer forensics have developed advanced systems which are used to collect evidence from computer systems without tampering with the evidence.

Computer forensics is a specialised field and has legal implications when investigating and collecting evidence. It is a recommendation that IS audit teams make use of experts when working on IS audits which require forensic investigations.

Cloud Computing Security Auditing

Cloud computing is a new IT solution which is growing in terms of usage. Many enterprises that would like to cut costs and also move away from administering large and complex IT systems have taken up cloud computing services. Cloud computing is growing in popularity and is considered by many enterprises to be a better option than managing an IT infrastructure themselves.

Application systems can be run from the cloud in a similar way an enterprise would run application systems from the local data centre. Most enterprises using cloud computing services have moved most of their core application systems, such as ERP and email systems into the cloud.

The major concern with cloud computing is security. Many enterprises do not feel secure to have their data and information stored in the cloud with many other enterprises located on the same virtual servers. Whilst the concern is rightly so, enterprises offering cloud services have gone an extra mile to ensure that client systems are secure. A client or enterprise using cloud computing is normally given its own virtual space on the cloud infrastructure which is secure and only available to a specific enterprise. Cloud solution providers also offer dedicated physical servers to host application systems and data.

Auditing a cloud computing infrastructure would require a good understanding of the security architecture and systems used to run the infrastructure. This would help the IS audit team understand how security is implemented by the cloud service provider. The first audit objective would be to assess security at the hosting site. Secondly, the audit team might consider reviewing security for application systems, data, and other systems the enterprise has on the cloud computing platform. The review would include access controls, disaster recovery, web server security, and data protection.

Standards have been developed for implementing cloud computing security such as ISO 27017. This new standard is based on ISO 27002. Most cloud computing service providers have also developed their own internal security standards. ISACA has also developed guidelines for auditing cloud computing security.

Auditing security on a cloud computing platform would require the use of a combination of tools which could include checklists and questionnaires for testing security compliance. The IS audit team might also consider using software interrogation tools which can be used to test various technologies used by the service providers. Key technologies include virtualization servers, network infrastructure, database systems, physical storage, and application systems.

The challenges of security in a cloud computing platform are many, and security should be managed effectively and proactively with the active involvement of client enterprises. Service providers can only go up to a certain limit in terms of providing security. Providing security training to users is a key aspect of securing systems on the cloud platform. User awareness training is an important security component as fraud and data theft has been perpetuated by employees.

A robust internal security system is critical to the successful implementation of a secure environment in the enterprise. The cloud service provider should also ensure that their environment is secure and cannot be easily penetrated.

Cloud computing will be one of the major IT services in the near future, and IS auditors need to prepare for this new development in terms of acquiring new skills. The use of cloud computing experts will grow, and the demand for such experts will also grow.

Auditing Databases

One common audit which often requires the use of other experts is database auditing. Many database systems used by large enterprises are complex and integrated with other databases and application systems. In order to get good results and if the audit is highly technical, it is recommended to use other experts who have the required qualifications and competencies.

Technical database system audits would require reviewing the structure of the database, application system and database account mapping, data integrity checks, database security, data tables, queues, triggers, object storage, and use of alerts and queries. How these features are configured differ from one database to the other. The configuration in Oracle databases will not be the same as in MS-SQL databases. So an expert in Oracle will be more suitable to provide expert services on an Oracle database infrastructure audit.

Audit objectives will cover technical aspects of the database as indicated above. Management might also include performance of the database, and the expert might be required to use defined metrics to assess performance of the database.

There are various standards and guidelines which can be used to audit a database system. ISACA has developed IS audit guidelines for databases. You will also find various types of standards for securing and configuring databases. Individual enterprises do also develop internal guidelines, which they normally use to configure and administer databases.

Database experts can make use of various tools to audit database. The tools allow the expert to extract and analyse data and data structures. The expert can also analyse information in audit trails and other reporting tools.

Auditing databases can be a big and challenging task, and depending on the size and structure of the databases, the IS audit team may require the use of more than one expert. Some enterprises have implemented multiple databases, and each database has a specific function. Where security and system recovery is a major concern, some enterprises have implemented failover databases and replication servers.

Auditing Firewalls

Firewalls are designed to secure the internal networks from outside threats, and regular audits are recommended in order to ensure that firewalls are providing the required security. Due to changes in firewall configuration in the course of IT operations, it is possible that new vulnerability may be introduced. Many times hackers also try to penetrate our firewalls using known firewall ports such as port 8080 for Internet traffic.

Auditing firewalls require a good understanding of firewall software and how the devices are configured. Less skilled auditors can access the firewalls using web interfaces which are easy to use. An expert in firewalls is required to interpret the data being generated and posted to reporting tools by the firewalls. Many firewall monitoring tools can present data in graphical and table form which is easy to understand. Despite all these nice tools, there is still need for a firewall expert who can interpret the data and make appropriate conclusions and recommendations.

Firewalls can also be used to create demilitarised zones (DMZ) which are used to secure IT systems which sit between the internal network and the public. Servers located in the DMZ are accessed by customers or the public without necessarily getting into the internal network. Firewalls can be installed using different designs and configurations depending on the services required.

Audit objectives for firewalls are mainly concerned with securing the internal network from external threats such as hackers and other unauthorised persons. It is also possible to use firewalls to perform routing functionality or to protect the internal network from viruses, malware, Trojans, and other intrusive rogue programs. Other audit objectives would include checking whether the firewalls are being monitored, recovery of a firewall in the event of a disaster, safe storage of firewall configuration, and replacement of firewall devices.

Firewalls can also be used to create VPN links with other offices such as branch offices or business partners. Where there are many branch offices and partners, the installation of firewall stacks may be complex and require an expert in firewalls to understand the architecture in order to carry out an effective IS audit.

There are various guidelines which are developed by firewall manufacturers for installing and operating firewall devices. The guidelines include how the firewall software should be configured. Many advanced firewalls use command line configuration, which require training to master in addition to using web interfaces.

The IS auditor should be aware that there are software- and hardware-based firewalls. There are also vendor-specific firewalls such as CISCO, Cyberoam, Check Point, and Fortinet. Each firewall type has its own standards. There are also generic standards which are developed by professional associations and standards organisations, such as the International Standards Organisation.

ISACA has developed guidelines which IS auditors can use to conduct firewall audits. The guidelines are generic and not specific to any vendor. The guidelines cover most common points which are found in most firewall configurations.

The expert can use various tools to audit firewalls, such as penetration testing tools, firewall monitors, and command line interrogation of the firewall.

The major challenge of firewalls is that there are many brands, and a firewall expert can only specialise in a few brands. It might be difficult to find experts for certain types of firewalls. This may make it difficult to perform a detailed and highly technical audit if the IS audit team cannot find a qualified and competent expert.

Since firewall configurations and installations can be complex, it is recommended to use firewall specialists as other experts to audit firewalls so that relevant data can be collected, analysed and appropriate conclusions and recommendations made.

SAP ERP System Auditing

SAP is a popular ERP system used by many enterprises worldwide. It is a powerful ERP system and able to produce good results for an enterprise. SAP requires good training to be able to use its functions effectively. The same applies to IS auditors who are assigned to audit the system. If the IS audit team does not have SAP-trained auditors, they will need to use other experts. These experts should have appropriate qualifications and competencies in SAP. The experts should also have experience in auditing or using SAP in order to perform an effective IS audit.

SAP as an ERP system is able to provide an end-to-end system which would automate most of the enterprise business processes. Common implementation of SAP includes modules such as material management, sales and distribution, finance and controlling, quality management, project systems, and human resources.

Audit objectives would include generic or highly technical tasks. Other audit objectives would include auditing input systems, processing systems, output systems, and integration between the application system and databases. The IS auditor would also be required to audit other databases linked to SAP ERP. It is always essential that effective controls are put in place which will ensure that there is data integrity when data is being transferred from one database to the other. The SAP ERP application has many features which the IS auditor needs to review.

SAP has its own standards, and ISACA has also developed standards for auditing SAP. The SAP standards and guidelines are more specific to the ERP application. An IS auditor would be effective in the audit if he made reference to both documents. The ISACA standard and guidelines will highlight the professional standards required to perform a successful SAP audit. The standards and guidelines from SAP will focus on how to configure and operate the application system.

The tools used to perform an IS audit on SAP would include compliance templates, data extraction tools, database analysis tools, and software interrogation tools. Audit trails and other system reporting tools are useful to the IS auditor as they contain a lot of important data.

The IS audit team, apart from making use of a SAP expert, can also make use of another expert. A data analyst or CAATs auditor can also be invited to carry out data investigations where the IS audit team would like to investigate further if the data on SAP contains errors, misposting, or fraud. The CAATs expert would perform investigations and analyse the data for any possible errors and make appropriate recommendations to the IS audit team.

The IS auditor requires good SAP technical skills and experience to be able to perform an effective audit which will achieve the objectives of the engagement. If the IS audit team does not have SAP skills, they can use other experts to provide SAP skills.

CAATs Auditing

CAATs auditing is the use of data analysis tools such as Excel, Audit Command Language (ACL), or IDEA to conduct investigations on data extracted from an application system or database. IS auditors would normally perform an IT general controls audit and, if they find material weakness in the controls, might decide to conduct further investigations by analysing data for errors or misposting.

CAATs can be used to analyse large amounts of data. The IS auditor does not need to take a sample but can use 100 per cent of the data because of the use of powerful workstations such as desktops and laptops we have at our disposal. IS auditors also have access to powerful servers which can be used to carry out analytics on large volumes of data.

The audit objective for CAATs is to check for errors in the data extracted from an application system. A skilled auditor or expert can use CAATs to investigate fraud or errors in data extracted. The

IS auditor using CAATs software can make a thorough analysis, put pieces of data together, and report significant findings if the data contains errors or incorrect information.

ISACA has developed guidelines for carrying out IS audits using CAATs. Tools which can be used to perform CAATs include ACL, IDEA, and Excel. CAATs can be conducted by IS auditors but require special analysis skills where large and complex data is involved.

Specialist Qualifications and Competencies

The specialist IS auditors are auditors who are, for example, CISA, CIA, or hold other IS audit qualifications. They also hold additional qualifications and competencies in specific areas of information systems. In most cases, these professionals would be what ISACA standard 1204.1 defines as other experts who are called to assist on an IS audit by providing skills and competencies not available on the IS audit team.

It is desirable that experts invited to assist the IS audit team have adequate competencies in order to achieve the engagement objectives. You may have noticed throughout our discussion in this chapter that we have referred to various competencies required to successfully perform an audit as an expert. Experience in previous audits should be considered as a good indicator of knowledge and skills required to successfully perform an IS audit. IS auditors who have had experience in similar audits are likely to be successful than those who have no previous background in providing IS auditing services in a particular specialist field.

Experts need to show their level of training on a particular system they have been selected to audit through their qualifications. Industry certifications are such qualifications which can be used to show the level of training. Enterprises such as Microsoft, CISCO,

Oracle, and SAP do provide training in their products for which candidates can be certified by sitting for examinations. The certification examinations are set at various levels from associate level to expert level.

Remember that it is the responsibility of the IS audit team to evaluate the qualifications and competencies of the experts who are providing professional services to the IS audit team. Evaluation of other experts can be based on qualifications, product skills, and experience.

Nature of Specialised Audits

As you have seen from what we have covered in this chapter so far, specialised audits are meant to address technical issues and require high-level skills. The selection of the right skills will ensure successful execution of the audit. Many times, audit teams have used less skilled and experienced IS auditors in order to cut costs. This has often resulted in poor results and heavy penalties on the IS audit team.

You have by now the understanding of specialised audits and when to use services of other experts to help in an IS audit engagement where the IS audit team does not have the required skills.

REFERENCES

Using ITFA, ITFA 2nd edition, 2013, ISACA, page 6

1401 reporting, ITAF 2nd edition, 2013, ISACA, page 37

1200 series standards statements, ITAF 2nd edition, 2013, ISACA, pages 12–39

CISA Study Guide, ISACA, 2012

The Path to IT audit, Shawna Scharf, *Internal Auditor Journal*, October 2012

The IS Audit Process. S. Anantha Sayana, ISACA Journal, 2002

ISO/IEC 27001:2013 Standard, Information security

Information Systems Governance, University of Victoria, December, 2006

COBIT 5 for Information Security, ISACA, 2013

Board briefing on IT governance, 2nd edition, ISACA, 2003

COBIT 5 Framework, ISACA, 2012

ISO/IEC 31000:2009, Risk Management Standard, ISO

ISO/IEC 27005:2011, Information Security Risk Management, ISO

COBIT 5 for Risk framework, ISACA, 2013

COBIT 5 for Information Security, ISACA, 2013

ISO 38500:2008, IT Governance Standard, ISO

ISO 22301: 2012, Business Continuity, ISO

ISO/IEC 27014:2013, Information Security Governance, ISO

ISO/IEC 24762:2008, Disaster Recovery Management, ISO

ISO/IEC 27037:2012, Forensic Digital Evidence, ISO

INDEX

A

B

C

D

E

F

G

H

I

L

M

N

O

P

Q

R

S

T

U

V

W

www.ingramcontent.com/pod-product-compliance
Lightning Source LLC
Chambersburg PA
CBHW051224050326
40689CB00007B/793
* 9 7 8 1 4 9 0 7 5 4 9 9 4 *